PAUL VI

People of God

Remarkable Lives, Heroes of Faith

People of God is a series of inspiring biographies for the general reader. Each volume offers a compelling and honest narrative of the life of an important twentieth- or twenty-first-century Catholic. Some living and some now deceased, each of these women and men has known challenges and weaknesses familiar to most of us but responded to them in ways that call us to our own forms of heroism. Each offers a credible and concrete witness of faith, hope, and love to people of our own day.

More titles to follow . . .

Paul VI

Pilgrim Pope

Michael Collins

LITURGICAL PRESS
Collegeville, Minnesota
www.litpress.org

Cover design by Stefan Killen Design. Cover illustration by Philip Bannister.

1   2   3   4   5   6   7   8   9

Library of Congress Control Number: 2017958486

ISBN 978-0-8146-4669-4   978-0-8146-4693-9 (e-book)

Contents

Preface

On Sunday, June 30, 1963, just nine days after his election as pope, Giovanni Battista Montini composed his Last Will and Testament. Earlier that day he had been crowned pope on the balcony of St. Peter's Basilica, the 262nd successor to St. Peter as Bishop of Rome and the last pope to wear the triple tiara. The arduous ceremony, which had lasted some three hours, brought to a conclusion the process of election that had begun with the death of Pope John XXIII on June 3.

As he wrote in neat copperplate handwriting, Pope Paul recalled the key figures of his life. In his mind's eye he could see his parents, his brothers, and a multitude of friends who had accompanied him throughout his life.

> I feel obliged to thank and to bless those who were the means of conveying to me the gifts of life received from thee O Lord: those who brought me into life (Oh! blessed be my most worthy parents!), those who educated me, loved me, did good to me, helped me, surrounded me with good examples, with care, affection, trust, goodness, kindness, friendship, fidelity and deference. I look with gratitude on the natural and spiritual relationships which have given origin, assistance, support, significance to my humble existence: how many gifts, how many beautiful and noble

things, how much hope have I received in this world! Now that my day is drawing to a close, and all of this stupendous and dramatic temporal and earthly scene is ending and dissolving, how can I further thank thee, O Lord, after the gift of natural life, also for the higher gift of faith and grace, in which alone at the end my surviving existence finds refuge?[1]

CHAPTER ONE

The Birth and Youth of John Baptist Montini

The small rural town of Concesio lies some eight kilometers north of Brescia in the Trompia valley. Concesio had its origins in the early medieval period, and a Christian population existed already in the sixth century. The town expanded rapidly in the sixteenth century when many Brescian nobles bought land and built houses in the hamlet. While not taking up permanent residence, the country villas offered members of the noble families a pleasant escape from Brescia during the suffocating summers.

It was in such a villa, one that had formerly belonged to the noble family of Lodron, that Giovanni Battista Montini was born on September 26, 1897. His father, Giorgio Montini (1860–1943), was some fourteen years older than his mother, Giuditta Alghisi (1874–1943). His father's family had acquired the large summer house and adjacent land in 1863. In the latter stages of her pregnancy Giuditta Alghisi traveled to their country farmhouse on the Via Vantini at Concesio to prepare for the birth of her second child. Her

1

first son, Ludovico, had been born a little over a year earlier on May 8, 1896, at the main family house in Brescia. Given the intense summer heat in the city, Giuditta came to spend the last months of her pregnancy in the countryside.

Giuditta was twenty-three when she gave birth to her second son. She had met her future husband on the steps of St. Peter's Basilica five years earlier when Giuditta was just eighteen. The two were independently on pilgrimage to Rome. Although she always recalled that their meeting was "love at first sight," she had to wait until she was twenty-one before marriage could be considered with the permission of her father.

The couple married on August 1, 1895, in the church of San Nazzaro in Brescia, and the reception took place in the bride's family home. Giorgio had graduated from the faculty of jurisprudence at the University of Padua, but he chose to pursue a career in journalism. Although only twenty-one years old, he was appointed editor by a Brescia-based attorney, Giuseppe Tovini, of the newly founded *Il Cittadino di Brescia*.

Giorgio's profession was somewhat avant-garde. However, the daily Catholic newspaper quickly established itself in a country that was struggling to cope with rapid change on the political front. When the Papal States were confiscated by the newly established Italian government in 1871, Pope Pius IX (1846–78) withdrew to the enclave of the Vatican. A myopic decision by the Holy See to dissuade Catholics from voting in elections resulted in some three decades when the political scene developed with few references to the Christian faith. In particular, it allowed the expansion of Freemasonry in Italian politics, schools, and universities. Despite the limitations, the church continued to provide hospitals, nursing homes, schools, and other social services for the general population, which remained resolutely Catholic.

Toward the end of the nineteenth century, the Italian peninsula underwent enormous changes. For centuries the country had been divided into duchies, city-states, kingdoms, and republics. Two-thirds of the population subsisted on the land while the remaining third lived in cities and major towns. By the fin de siècle the population was close to 30 million, although some 200,000 emigrated each year to other parts of Europe or the New World.

The average age of Italian citizens was forty-two, although infant mortality was high with 20 percent of infants dying before their first birthday. Space was often limited, as extended members of the family often lived in small houses made of brick or stone. Malnutrition was widespread as were associated diseases. Running water was confined to the houses of the middle class and wealthy, while the poor shared water from wells.

Although the country had been officially united into the Kingdom of Italy in 1871, the process of unification was slow, and many citizens remained loyal to their previous rulers. Dialect was slow to change and efforts to standardize the Italian language proved difficult. The polite and familiar grammatical forms of address reflected a class society based on money, political influence, and privilege. The church, with its two-thousand-year-old traditions, reinforced the maintenance of the status quo. The poor sat on one side of the church, while the well off occupied the central pews. It was into this society that the Montini children were born.

Four days after his birth, on September 30, the infant was baptized Giovanni Battista—John the Baptist—in the local parish church at Concesio. He was the fifteenth child to have been born in the parish that year.

Giuditta's pregnancy had been difficult. On the advice of her mother-in-law, Francesca Buffali, Giuditta sent the newborn to a wet nurse who lived some six kilometers away at Bovezzo. Twenty-three-year-old Corinda Peretti, who had three children of her own, kept the young Giovanni Battista in her home for several months. When the young boy finally returned to the family, he was brought to the main residence at Via Dante in Brescia.

Life remained tranquil for the young child. The third and last child in the family, Francesco, was born on September 22, 1900. Summer vacations were taken each year in both Concesio and Verolavecchia, the latter an isolated village to the south of Brescia where Giuditta had family. During the winter months Ludovico, Giovanni Battista, and Francesco remained at home with their mother and entertained their numerous cousins. At the age of six Giovanni Battista followed his elder brother to the local Jesuit-run Collegio Cesare Arici. It was an obvious choice, for in 1899 the family had moved to Via Trieste 37, just a block away from the school.

The young Giovanni Battista settled into school and his teachers and contemporaries later recalled Giovanni Battista as a quiet and reserved youth, pious and committed to learning. The years of formal schooling were often interrupted by periods of ill health, although this rarely disrupted his education. On June 6, 1907, the young Giovanni Battista made his First Communion at the chapel of the Sisters of the Holy Child in Brescia.

The brothers did well at the Jesuit school, their education amplified by the stories their parents read to them at bedtime. In 1907 the family made a pilgrimage to Rome, where they spent a few days visiting St. Peter's and the principal churches and shrines of the city. They returned to Brescia, where, some weeks later, both Ludovico and Giovanni Battista received their First Communion and the sacrament of confirmation.

Shortly afterward the family moved house for the last time, taking up residence at Via Grazie 7, just across the street from the church of Santa Maria della Grazie. Here the boys became altar servers and also frequented the nearby church of the Oratorians, Santa Maria della Pace. It was at this church that the young Giovanni Battista met one of the most influential people in his life. Father Giulio Bevilacqua joined the oratory shortly after his ordination in June 1908 and was assigned to the oratory of Santa Maria della Pace. The quiet and taciturn Montini was fascinated by this somewhat rumbustious young priest. Another young cleric, Paolo Caresana, also joined the oratory in 1912 and became the spiritual director and confessor to the young Giovanni Battista. The Oratorians had a particular apostolate to young people and invited youths to accompany them on their cycling trips into the countryside. The young Giovanni Battista developed a passion for cycling and regularly joined the weekly excursions. Such popular activities engaged young people but also fostered vocations to the priesthood and religious life. In keeping with the times, these engagements were designed for young men rather than women.

At the age of sixteen Giovanni Battista left the Jesuit school to conclude his formal education at home. Although he was officially enrolled in the Liceo Arnaldo da Brescia, he rarely attended classes. A bout of ill health prevented him from continuing with his companions, and the decision was made to provide a private tutor. During the summer Giovanni Battista had suffered an unspecified malady, the culmination of two years of health concerns for his parents. While cycling one day, the teenage Montini collapsed, alerting his doctor to possible cardiac problems. The trauma affected the young man, who could not understand his precarious bouts of ill health and fatigue.

World War I began on July 28, 1914, and Pope Pius X (1903–14) died almost a month later on August 20. As he neared the end of his education, Giovanni Battista contemplated what path he would choose for his future professional career. His earliest intention was to become a writer or a journalist like his father. To this end he considered studying Italian literature at university. He also examined a possible vocation to the Benedictine way of life. From this he was dissuaded by a Benedictine monk, Dom Denys Buenner, who believed that Montini was not sufficiently robust to withstand the privations of monastic life. He also spoke to his favorite priest at the Jesuit school, Fr. Persico, about his hopes to be a priest. At the age of nineteen Giovanni Battista graduated from the *liceo* with the highest marks possible.

Around this time Giovanni Battista met a newly ordained priest who had recently been appointed assistant pastor at Concesio. Don Francesco Galloni, just twenty-four, arrived in the small town full of plans to stir up the quiet parish. The urbane young priest was extremely popular and visited the family often. The Montinis had gone up a notch on the social ladder the previous year when Giorgio was appointed *assessore*, an unelected position for local political oversight, to the township of Brescia.

If coverage of the war occupied Giorgio's time and energy in 1914, it redoubled when Italy entered the war in May of the following year. Initially Italy had been allied to both Germany and the Austro-Hungarian Empire. This Triple Alliance had been intended as a purely defensive measure in the event that one of its members was attacked. But as the other two had started war without Italy's approval, the latter had avoided confrontation. By early summer 1915, however, Italy opted to side with Germany against the Austro-Hungarian Empire.

Suddenly the war was on everybody's lips. The nearby Austrians, once friendly neighbors, were now belligerents. The war spread into northern Italy, dividing families and communities. The Oratorian house at La Pace in Brescia was taken by the Italian authorities and turned into a field hospital. In 1915 Ludovico Montini joined the army and was sent to a military Aviation Corps while Giovanni Battista concluded his final state exams.

After a brief summer vacation at Viareggio, Giovanni Battista returned home, where his family anxiously awaited news about Ludovico's fate. As the war gathered momentum, Giovanni Battista presumed that it would be only a matter of time before he was conscripted for military service. In early September Giorgio took Giovanni Battista to Rome on a business trip. During the visit, the teenager confided to his father his hopes to enter the seminary if he were not drafted for military service. Given Giovanni Battista's precarious health, however, it was uncertain that he would be enlisted.

Plans for the seminary were also affected by the war. The traditional opening date for Italian seminaries was in the second half of October. Most had suspended their intake of young students because of the war, however, and some seminaries had been commandeered during the hostilities by the Italian government. The bishops did not want to be accused of harboring young men fleeing conscription. Accordingly, Bishop Giacinto Gaggia of Brescia granted the seminarians permission to attend philosophy and theology classes while residing at home.

As he had suspected—and to his mother's relief—Giovanni Battista was rejected by the army on health grounds. News of the capture of Don Giulio Bevilacqua, who had been serving as an army chaplain, perturbed him, as did reports of other companions who were imprisoned by the enemy. The war had entered Italian soil, and the hostilities rapidly worsened. A constant concern was for the safety of Rome, which the Italians feared would eventually fall to the invaders.

Pope Benedict XV (1914–22) regularly condemned the war as a doomed enterprise for which he was loudly condemned by all the belligerents. In October 1917 Giovanni Battista accompanied his father once more to Rome. Giorgio had begun to take a prominent role in Italian politics and was appointed president of the Unione Popolare, a predecessor of Catholic Action, which was founded in 1927. This was a position given personally by Pope Pius XI and indicated the pontiff's esteem for Giorgio Montini. Yet within the year he had to resign as he found it impossible to divide his time between Brescia and Rome.

The Great War finally concluded with an armistice on November 11, 1918. At the eleventh hour of the eleventh day of the eleventh month the guns fell silent. The war, which had lasted four years and four months, had claimed some eighteen million lives. The arrival of the United States had convinced Germany and her allies that they could not win the war. A treaty, prepared largely by Britain and France, was signed by all parties at Versailles on June 28, 1919.

Since his election, Pope Benedict XV had pragmatically encouraged lay Catholics to play a greater role in Italian society. The period since 1870 had been characterized by hostility between the Italian government and the Vatican authorities. Benedict wished to normalize church–state relations, and he understood that negotiation was necessary. But first he wanted to strengthen the role of Catholics in the political life of the country; otherwise, he feared, the country could be ruled by either fascists or communists. Given that the majority of Italians were Catholic, it made sense to encourage their participation in public and political life.

Papal support for the emergence of Catholics into Italian political life was further enhanced when Benedict XV gave permission to a remarkable Sicilian priest, Luigi Sturzo, to found a political party, the Partitio Popolare Italiano (Italian People's Party). Giorgio Montini was among those who successfully stood for public office at the elections in November 1919. In that same month Giovanni Battista made his last preparations for ordination to the priesthood. He received the soutane, the ankle-length coat worn by seminarians and clerics. On February 28, 1920, he was ordained subdeacon and three months later, on May 29, Giovanni Battista was ordained a priest, along with thirteen companions in the cathedral of Brescia.

CHAPTER TWO

The Call to Rome

The day after his ordination ceremony Giovanni Battista celebrated his first Mass at the church of Santa Maria della Grazie. His mother watched with pride as he donned the white chasuble that she had made from her own wedding dress. Throughout the rest of his life Don Battista returned regularly to the church, celebrating Mass on 232 occasions—the last of which was days before the conclave that elected him as pope.

Shortly after his first Mass, the young priest accompanied his father to Rome, where both were received in a semi-private audience by Pope Benedict XV. The political situation in Italy was complex, with factions divided into anarchists, communists, and fascists. The latter were growing increasingly powerful, and the pope was concerned about the curtailing of the privileged position of the Catholic Church.

At the unusually young age of twenty-two, Giovanni Battista was now a priest of the historic Diocese of Brescia. Although many of the diocese's four hundred parishes had vacancies, Bishop Giacinto Gaggia decided to send the young Don Giovanni Battista to Rome for further studies.

This was due partly to his studious nature and partly to his precarious health. During the summer months he was assigned to the rural parish of Veralanuova in the suburbs of Brescia. On November 10 Don Giovanni arrived in Rome to begin studies in literature and history, enrolling in an introductory course in classical Greek and Latin literature in the city's Sapienza University. The young cleric took up lodgings in the Lombard College, a regional seminary and house for postgraduate studies for clergy from the north of Italy. Here he enrolled in literature and contemporaneously began studies in theology at the Jesuit-run Gregorian College.

This was to be the young priest's first experience of communal life, having avoided the discipline of seminary life due to the residential exemptions made during the war. He found it difficult to settle into a routine, engaging little with his fellow clerics and devoting himself to his studies. Even so, he found the rhythm of the college challenging and difficult.

Giovanni Battista had family company in Rome as his brother Ludovico had enrolled in the faculty of law at the university. The two brothers rarely met for both were engaged in their studies, although they sent letters to each other every few days. Their father, increasingly immersed in Italian politics, paid regular visits to Rome. Gaining permission to be absent from the college for a meal with his father was difficult for the young Montini.

One of the advantages of living in Rome was not simply a deeper understanding of the classical world that he was studying but also that of contemporary Italian politics. Through their father, the Montinis came to know the family of Giovanni Longinotti. The latter was the undersecretary of the Ministry of Commerce and Labor, an important position in postwar Italy.

It was due to Longinotti's influence that the young priest's life changed dramatically. During a casual conversation with Cardinal Pietro Gasparri, secretary of state to Pope Benedict XV, Longinotti mentioned the young Montini. In a country where formal recommendations count more than merits, a word from a distinguished politician carried weight. Gasparri investigated Montini's record with the college rector and was pleased to receive a positive assessment of the young cleric.

On October 27, 1921, the young Don Battista was called to the Apostolic Palace overlooking St. Peter's Basilica. At Gasparri's direction he had been summoned by Monsignor Giuseppe Pizzardo, the substitute secretary who oversaw the internal workings of the Holy See. After a few pleasantries, Pizzardo explained to his visitor his intention to suggest his enrollment in the Academy for Noble Ecclesiastics, the Holy See's school for diplomats. Montini was astonished at the proposal and expressed his amazement. Pizzardo told him to do nothing for the moment while the consent from his bishop in Brescia was formalized. Although he did not protest to Pizzardo, he lamented in letters to his parents that his hope was to return to Brescia and work in a parish.

Permission to study at the Pontifical Academy was granted by the bishop of Brescia and the young priest transferred from the Lombard College to the Academy in the Palazzo Severoli at the Piazza della Minerva, directly across from the Dominican church of Santa Maria della Minerva.

The diplomatic service of the Holy See is the oldest in the world. Some historians trace its origins to the delegation sent by Pope Sylvester (314–35) to represent him at the Council of Nicea in 325. The present academy traces its roots to Pope Clement XI (1700–21), who authorized Abbot Pietro Garagni to set up the school in 1701. The front of the palazzo had been demolished by Napoleon's troops at the end of the eighteenth century but the building was still an imposing edifice that overlooked the second-century Pantheon.

Accustomed to the discipline of the Lombard College, Montini found himself once more in a rigid scholastic atmosphere. Although all his colleagues were priests, the regime was demanding, and free time was limited. Giovanni Battista began further studies in canon law and learned three foreign languages. The college had been founded principally for the priest-sons of noble families who were destined to enter the diplomatic service of the Holy See. Even in the twenty-first century, its rules and regulations remained much as they had been in the eighteenth.

Each week Giovanni Battista wrote to his parents, sharing the news from Rome and responding to their correspondence. His health was a constant theme but he assured his mother that he was in good shape. With his father he discussed the developing political situation. The letters give us a clear insight into the mind of the young Giovanni Battista at a critically formative time in his young life and indicate his fascination with politics.

Shortly into the new year, an event occurred that was to change Montini's life once more. While waiting in a drafty corridor in the Vatican for a doorman to find a key, Pope Benedict had caught a severe chill. He had just celebrated Mass at the nearby Domus Sanctae Marthae and had insisted on walking to the Apostolic Palace in the rain. He took to bed and developed pneumonia. Some days later, on January 22, he died of complications at the age of sixty-seven.

After the papal funeral, the cardinals were ensconced in the Sistine Chapel to elect a new pope. On February 6, 1922, a fellow Lombard, Cardinal Achille Ratti, emerged as Pope Pius XI (1922–39). Montini had met the cardinal a few times before his election. Ratti, born in the town of Desio in the province of Milan, was an academic who had served most of his life as librarian of the Ambrosian Library and, more recently, the Vatican Library. A noted scholar, Ratti was more pugnacious than his predecessor. Although he had spent his life in academia, Ratti had a sharp interest in Italian politics.

On March 6 the new pope received students from the Pontifical Academy at the Apostolic Palace. There was no address during the semiprivate audience, just the exchange of a few pleasantries. When Pius met the young Montini, he asked him to pass on his regards to his father. It was a tacit papal endorsement for his father, who had been elected to the Italian parliament as a deputy.

The arrival of Pius to the papal throne corresponded to a dramatic shift in Italian politics. On October 31, 1922, the leader of the Socialist Party, Benito Mussolini, had become prime minister, an office that he would occupy for the next twenty-one years. Montini had just returned to Rome from a study period in Germany when he received a note from Monsignor Pizzardo requesting that he return to Brescia to conclude his doctorate in canon law at the seminary of Milan.

Having completed his studies, Montini returned to Rome expecting to enter the Academy as soon as the new semester started. To his surprise, Pizzardo informed him that he would not enroll in the second semester but simply be resident in the Academy. The prelate gave no indication as to how long this unusual situation would last. To fill his time he could assist as an "auditor" in the classes held in the Academy without taking exams. The plan was to assign him as an assistant in a nunciature, an embassy of the Holy See.

By now Montini was having serious doubts about his ability as a diplomat. He had wanted to be a parish priest and accepted the request to pursue further studies in Rome only reluctantly. He wrote to his father expressing his frustration and anguish at the delay and confided that he did not feel well equipped.

His deliberations and doubts were cut short when a letter from Pizzardo assigned him to the nunciature in the Polish capital of Warsaw. Montini was appointed *addetto*, or office clerk, assisting Monsignor Carlo Chiarlo. The newly independent country was still recovering from the devastation of the First World War.

In early June 1923 Montini left Rome and took the train northward. After a brief stop to visit his parents in Brescia, he continued his journey through Vienna and on to Warsaw, arriving in the Polish capital on June 10. The horrors of the war were still visible throughout the tortured country as it struggled to deal with its new status. The new nation was one-third larger than prewar Poland. There were many nationals who belonged to ethnic minorities that had little if anything to do with the sovereign nation, and the process of assimilation was fraught with tension and difficulty.

The nunciature was located on Ksiazeka Street, beside the Church of St. Alexander. Archbishop Lorenzo Lauri welcomed the young cleric and assigned him to the opening of correspondence. Two months before Montini's arrival, Lauri had ratified a concordat between the Polish government and the Holy See. The negotiations had begun two years earlier and with the concordat in place, Lauri left Warsaw for Rome.

The young cleric began to learn Polish and was fascinated with the robust Catholicism and emerging sense of nationalism. His letters home showed little enthusiasm, however, for his new post. Vatican departments in Rome scaled back work to the minimum during the hot months of July and August. There was little correspondence, and that which arrived was none of Montini's concern. However, he reported that the staff members were kind, the food was Italian, and the weather was pleasantly warm. As a pastime, he wrote the occasional article for his father's newspaper. Montini continued to follow Italian politics closely. On July 11, 1923, just a month after Montini's arrival in Warsaw, Don Luigi Sturzo resigned as chairman of the Partitio Popolare Italiano that he had founded just four years earlier as an opposition party to the socialists. His departure was ordered by Cardinal Pietro Gasparri. Although Pope Benedict had tacitly approved the foundation, his successor, Pius XI, was skeptical of its effectiveness. As a Lombard, the new pope was native to the area in which the party was strongest, and he had come to mistrust its loyalty.

The Partitio Popolare Italiano was clearly anti-fascist, and Pius was exploring an accommodation with the party led by Mussolini. He therefore wished to prevent political friction while the Holy See made overtures to the fascists. It was the pope's intention to resolve the friction between the Holy See and the Italian government, which had its roots in the 1870s when Italy annexed the Papal States and confiscated ecclesiastical property, and he saw the fascists as the most pragmatic way of doing so. In the event, the decision was to split and ultimately weaken the Partitio Popolare Italiano.

Attacks on clergy became commonplace. On the night of August 23, Don Giovanni Minzoni, a priest from Ravenna, was clubbed to death by fascist supporters. His skull was smashed, and his lungs were punctured. The clergy of Italy had largely chosen to avoid conflict and persecution. Montini wrote to his father, expressing his concerns about the rise of fascism; in his reply, Giorgio noted that Catholics were afraid to allow their children to attend their parish churches for Holy Communion or confirmation instruction.

The rhythm of work at the Polish nunciature increased in September. The religious sisters who served the nunciature were concerned about Montini's health, due to the freezing winter months that would shortly descend upon northern Poland. Writing to his father, Giovanni Battista lamented that the days were melancholic, and the Polish language unpronounceable. He despaired of his time in Poland. His concerns were short lived for on October 2 he was summoned by a telegram from the cardinal secretary of state. Montini's father had used his influence to explain his concerns about his son's health.

Within a week Montini had packed his belongings, made his farewells, and set off for Rome. Once more he broke his journey in Brescia in order to spend a day with his parents. But by October 13 he returned to the Pontifical Academy. With elections due in April political tensions were rising. The ascent of the fascists, founded five years earlier, seemed inexorable. The Partitio Popolare Italiano, with Don Sturzo now in exile in London, continued to lose members.

The April elections saw the fascists gain a nearly unassailable position, but it was based on bullying, intimidation, and violence. The aftermath of the elections was marked with demonstrations and riots. In the midst of the political turmoil, Montini left Italy for a six-week break in France, where he intended to perfect his French and immerse himself in French culture. After a brief retreat with the Benedictines at Hautecombe in late July, Montini proceeded to Paris, where he enrolled in a language school. His first duty was to make a courtesy call at the newly acquired apostolic nunciature on Avenue Wilson. On August 9 a letter was forwarded to his residence on Rue Respaill from Cardinal Pietro Gasparri informing him that Montini would return to Rome in October and enter the Secretariat of State.

Montini may have suspected that such an appointment would come, for each year a number of young graduates were taken on at the central office of the Holy See.

But before this change came an intimate family celebration. His brother Ludovico had been engaged to be married to Giuseppina Folonari. Ludovico had graduated in law from the University of Padua, and on October 22, 1924, the young couple was married in the church of Santa Maria della Pace. At the nuptial Mass Giovanni Battista presided, wearing the white silk chasuble that had been made from their mother's bridal gown.

The following day Giovanni Battista traveled by train to Rome, where on October 25 he joined the group of graduates from the Academy at the Secretariat of State situated on the third floor of the sixteenth-century Apostolic Palace overlooking St. Peter's Basilica. This was to be his workplace for the next three decades. Starting once more as an *addetto*, or office clerk, he steadily advanced to the highest office short of the rank of secretary of state.

Giovanni Battista rented a small apartment on the Via Aurelia behind St. Peter's Basilica. Each morning he walked through a maze of small streets that led to the Vatican. Traversing St. Peter's Square he entered the Apostolic Palace through the bronze door in the colonnade designed by Gian Lorenzo Bernini in the seventeenth century. Ascending a series of stairs he reached the corridor decorated with sixteenth-century frescos of maps of the world. Entering the secretariat he took his place at a desk he shared with another colleague. A dossier of papers awaited him each morning to arrange, along with appointments to confirm, letters to draft, and documents to be read.

The Roman Curia was divided into a number of congregations, or offices, each of which administered particular aspects of the life of the church. The office of Propaganda Fidei, the Propagation of the Faith, oversaw the vast and rapidly expanding mission territories. Other offices oversaw diocesan bishops, priests, religious, the liturgy, and seminaries. While each was independent, all were answerable to the pontiff, who governed these through the Secretariat of State. Within the Secretariat was a section that dealt with the internal workings of the Vatican, while a second section administered international relations with foreign governments.

Montini arrived at the Vatican just two months before the jubilee year of 1925. On December 24, 1924, Pope Pius XI had inaugurated a holy year at St. Peter's Basilica. Over the course of the following twelve months, millions of pilgrims from around the world came to Rome. Pius knew that the influx of Catholics would have an impact on the political situation. The vast river of Catholics would remind the fascists of the spiritual power of the papacy. Accordingly, Ratti filled the year with events designed to underscore the role of the papacy on a global scale.

Although reserved by nature, Montini made friends among the several new recruits, many of whom were to remain friends for the rest of his life. Each day he came to a deeper understanding of the way the Holy See viewed the world and the complex mechanisms of the papal court. The Roman Curia was structured on the ancient *cursus honorum*, the career path the ancient Romans took through the army to public office. Rank and ecclesiastical titles were of supreme importance in an almost exclusively male world. The code of dress was governed by a Byzantine-like protocol. One's grade and rank was determined with a series of outmoded court titles and shades of dress that ranged from scarlet to amaranth. Moreover, the vast majority of those working in the Holy See were Italian.

The client–patron relationship was of crucial importance, for one could make progress in the grades of ecclesiastical honors only if one enjoyed the patronage of a senior prelate. Advancement was not always on merit; rather, it depended on personal relationships and contacts. Often external appearances and character were judged more important than intrinsic capability.

A year after his entry into the diplomatic service at the Secretariat, Montini was appointed *cameriere segreto supernumerario* with the title monsignor. He had passed the first grade and was now entitled to wear a purple sash and silk cape.

Although a diplomatic functionary, Montini was foremost a priest, and in 1925 he was nominated an ecclesiastical assistant or chaplain to the *Federazione Universitaria Cattolica Italiana* (FUCI), the federation of Italian Catholic university students founded in 1896. The recommendation to the Roman vicariate had come from Monsignor Pizzardo in the Roman Curia. Along with some other priests his responsibilities were to provide spiritual assistance to young Catholics. The association's headquarters were on the nearby Via della Scrofa.

In 1925 the young energetic Igino Rigetti was appointed president of the movement following a congress in Bologna, at which the congress had placed itself under the patronage of the king of Italy. This infuriated Pope Pius, who had not been consulted in advance and who then imposed Montini and Rigetti on the movement. Both men moved delicately to diffuse any resentment of the senior members of FUCI who jealously guarded their autonomy.

As a university group, meetings with students took place mainly throughout the thirty-week academic year. The annual activities began with a Mass in the Church of Santa

Maria della Minerva, and throughout the year various meetings were organized. Giovanni Battista was just twenty-eight years old, less than a decade older than most of the students. Initially he found difficulty in establishing a rapport with the young people, but he wrote regularly for student magazines and organized study groups where students could examine ethical questions and moral issues. He gradually came to know the students better and established a rapport and friendship with many that lasted for several years. It provided Montini with a welcome break from his Vatican duties, which tied him to a desk.

All this pastoral activity, however, was in his free time. Each day he attended the Secretariat of State from 8:00 a.m. until 2:00 p.m. and again from 5:00 p.m. until 8:00 p.m. While punctilious in his work, he accepted that he was simply a functionary charged with the activities of the lower echelons of government. Each week on Thursday afternoons he accompanied students to the poor area around Porta Metronia, where they assisted young children.

Living in the Eternal City had its compensations for the young cleric. He enjoyed exploring the art and architecture in which Rome abounded. Many of the greatest artists of the Renaissance and Baroque eras had transformed the city into a splendid showcase of Italian masterpieces. Michelangelo, Raphael, Bernini, and Bramante were among those employed by the popes to embellish the Eternal City. Gifted composers such as des Prez, Palestrina, Victoria, and Allegri had written for papal liturgies celebrated in the Sistine Chapel. On Sunday afternoons Giovanni Battista explored the churches and museums or strolled underneath the pines along the Via Appia Antica. Often he was accompanied by university students.

The FUCI was active in the university and retained a small headquarters close to the Pantheon. Gradually Montini found himself drawn deeper into the work of the chaplaincy, and he developed a strong friendship with Igino Rigetti, six years his junior. While Rigetti was spontaneous and optimistic, Montini was cautious and reserved. The two edited a weekly newspaper for students called *La Sapienza*. The chaplaincy was always busy with students who, despite the cramped conditions, found the congenial atmosphere a pleasant refuge from the university. Rigetti and Montini both had a desk surrounded by books.

The Italian political situation, however, continued to deteriorate. The fascists were determined to seize power at whatever cost. In October 1926 a fifteen-year-old boy was shot dead for attempting to kill Mussolini. The production of newspapers, including Montini's *Cittadino di Brescia*, was often disrupted. Montini regularly intervened to dissuade students from violent skirmishes with the fascists. Yet despite his work in the Secretariat of State, Giovanni Battista was largely unaware of the rapprochement between the Holy See and the fascists.

Following the unification of Italy in the late nineteenth century, Rome became the capital of the new kingdom. The Papal States, territories that had belonged to the papacy since the eighth century, were absorbed along with other small duchies, republics, and city-states that had made up the Italian peninsula since the fall of the Roman Empire in Western Europe in 476. Pope Pius IX had vehemently opposed the confiscation of the Papal States and successive popes had tried to come to an agreement with the Italian authorities.

From 1926 onwards, Cardinal Gasparri and representatives of King Victor Emmanuel III held a series of negotiations, which culminated in the successful conclusion to the vexed problem. On February 11, 1929, Cardinal Gasparri, representing the pope, and Benito Mussolini, representing the king, signed an agreement at the Lateran Palace. Under the terms of the agreement, Vatican City State was established, giving the papacy the right to 144 acres around St. Peter's, along with extraterritorial properties, and financial compensation for the properties seized seven decades earlier. In addition, the Italian authorities recognized Catholicism as the religion of the majority of the nation. The agreement finally allowed Catholics to fully participate in the political and cultural life of Italy. The initial euphoria surrounding the agreement did not last long, however. Within months Pope Pius complained that Mussolini had taken advantage of his goodwill and was not serious in his intent to make proper restitution for properties confiscated seven decades earlier.

Of greater consequence was the political situation in northern Europe. The dismantling of the German, Russian, Austro-Hungarian, and Ottoman Empires in the early decades of the twentieth century had left lacunae to be filled. The emergence of smaller states and the redrawing of borders created a migration crisis in the heartland of Europe. Germany had been humiliated under the terms of the 1919 Treaty of Versailles and had suffered a severe economic decline. The army had been reduced to 100,000 soldiers. It was from this political turmoil that the young Austrian soldier Adolf Hitler emerged to gather popular support for his plans to reassert Germany as a superpower on the map of Europe.

For three years Eugenio Pacelli, later Pope Pius XII (1939–58), had served as nuncio to Bavaria before moving as nuncio to Prussia (and virtually all of Germany) in 1920. From Berlin he served as the ambassador of the Holy See for ten years. A Germanophile, Pacelli negotiated concordats between the Holy See and the German and Prussian governments. Returning to Rome in 1929, Pacelli was regarded as highly successful in his diplomatic achievements. He was created a cardinal in December of that same year, and two months later he replaced Cardinal Gasparri as secretary of state, thus becoming Montini's new supervisor. Pacelli was highly regarded by Pope Pius XI. Although fiercely independent, the elderly pontiff increasingly relied on Pacelli's sage advice. Pacelli's manner soothed the pope, who became more irascible with age. Despite Pacelli's political negotiations, cracks in the relationship between the fascist government and the church widened rapidly. The government criticized several Catholic youth movements for a lack of patriotism, and at the end of May 1931 suppressed all Catholic youth movements, including FUCI. The Holy See appeared to support the closure by transferring such organizations to the care of the local bishop, which effectively meant that Montini would cease in his role as national chaplain. Montini had, in the meantime, been appointed to teach ecclesiastical history at the Pontifical Academy, where he had studied papal diplomacy some years earlier.

In late June Pope Pius completed and published a political encyclical. Entitled *Non Abbiamo Bisongno* (We Have No Need), the document contained a ringing denunciation of Mussolini for his closure of the Catholic youth groups of Italy. Despite the Lateran Treaty signed two years earlier that separated the church and state, the pope condemned Italian fascists of neopaganism. Pius knew that Mussolini would not allow the free distribution of the encyclical in Italy and entrusted some members of the Curia to deliver it outside Italian territories. The young Montini was sent to deliver the document to the nuncio in Munich. It was the nuncio's task to have the encyclical printed and distributed in the staunchly Catholic Bavaria.

Pacelli summoned Giovanni Battista to his office and informed the young priest that in the future he was to concentrate his efforts on his work at the Secretariat and wind down his work with FUCI. Several months later Monsignor Pizzardo officially confirmed the end of his chaplaincy.

Giovanni Battista was deeply distressed. Over the decade working with the young students he had made many friends. Despite the conclusion of his formal responsibilities, however, he continued to celebrate Mass and preach each Sunday at Sapienza University. He also organized weekend retreats for young people at the Abbey of St. Paul Outside-the-Walls, where his host was Abbot Ildefonso Schuster, who would later become archbishop of Milan. Montini was also spiritual director to the small group of FUCI members who joined the St. Vincent de Paul Society, met at the Augustinian house of St. Anne at the Vatican, and worked in the poor area of Primavalle. Montini also published three small booklets on Christ during the period. In 1936 he set up a series of seminars for the men of the FUCI confederation.

Work at the Secretariat consumed the vast majority of his time. Although the Curia was organized by Pope Sixtus V (1585–90) in the late sixteenth century, its origins lay in the ashes of the Roman Empire. The ancient Curia allowed men to enter civil service whose highest goal was to serve in the Senate or to take a high military command. The stages of progress were strictly laid down. As the candidate matured, evermore senior offices were assigned. These were governed by titles and positions of power. From the medieval period the College of Cardinals rather than the senate was the goal for clergy who made their careers in the papal civil service. While much of the Curia was effective, it suffered from stagnation. Cardinals had no retirement age and some remained in office after they were no longer physically or mentally able to carry out their duties. Junior members in the ranks were sometimes noted for their leaden approach as they waited to see which patrons they should follow in the shifting sea of curial appointments. In many ways it was an old boys' club playing with outdated rules.

Pope Pius was convinced of the importance of concordats between various European countries with a strong Catholic culture. During his pontificate some eighteen concordats were signed between international governments to promote and protect the rights of the church. While all eventually failed in the face of the oncoming global war, Pius believed that they were the best bulwark in the uncertain political climate. Yet these concordats were often negotiated without the agreement of the local episcopate or population.

With Pacelli's arrival, Montini was offered lodgings in the Vatican overlooking the sixteenth-century Belvedere Court-yard. He had hitherto occupied a small villa on the Aventine Hill, which he shared with some paying guests, including his friend Fr. Giulio Bevilacqua. Situated on a slight rise overlooking the Tiber and the Circus Maximus, the villa had been an oasis of peace. The large apartment at the Vatican was a dramatic change.

In the summer of 1933 Montini temporarily replaced the *sostituto* Monsignor Domenico Tardini during the latter's annual vacation. It was a signal of Cardinal Pacelli's confidence in his proficiency as a diplomat. Montini continued his friendships with former FUCI students. Several had married and invited him to various family celebrations. But his office at FUCI no longer existed, and there was no place to meet the students who were now bereft of the spiritual care offered by the church.

Montini used his vacation time to travel outside Italy. In 1934 he toured Scotland and England. These brought him into firsthand contact with Anglican worship, an experience that would prove important years later when as pope he sought to improve ecumenical relations with the churches of the Reformation.

From his position at the Secretariat of State Giovanni Battista watched dramatic changes unfold throughout central Europe. Despite the series of concordats so dear to Pius and Pacelli's hearts, the continent was changing. If atheistic communism was perceived as the Russian threat, the rise of fascism and nationalism was of equal concern.

In 1935 Mussolini tried to appropriate Abyssinia, present-day Ethiopia. The following year Spain was engulfed in a civil war following an uprising led by General Francisco Franco. The nationalists had been infuriated by the replacement of the monarch by a republic in 1931, precipitating a war that dragged on until 1939, taking half a million lives with it.

The overriding preoccupation at the Vatican during this period was the civil war in Spain, the inexorable rise of fascism in Italy, and the aggressive march of Nazism in Germany. On March 10, 1937, Pope Pius published his encyclical *Mit Brennender Sorge* (With Burning Heart), in which he objected to the breaches of the 1933 concordat by the German government. The first draft of the encyclical was composed by Cardinal Faulhaber, who cautioned the pope against naming the Nazi party in his condemnation.

Later that year Domenico Tardini was appointed secretary for the Extraordinary Affairs at the Secretariat of State. Tardini had begun his work at the Secretariat of State in 1929, and Montini had become a trusted friend and colleague. At the time Montini held the post of *primo minutante*, or chief drafter of documents. When absent from the office, Tardini asked Montini to replace him. As a result, Montini came into increasing contact with Cardinal Pacelli.

Tardini's promotion at the end of the year provided a promotion for Montini as *sostituto*, literally the substitute secretary of state who oversaw the internal running of the Curia. Both Pope Pius and Cardinal Pacelli were indefatigable workers, rising early and retiring late. Montini's promotion was broadly welcomed by the modest staff that administered the Curia. His ability for work became legendary. When the staff left the office at 8:00 p.m. each evening, Montini returned to his office after supper to continue administering paperwork until he retired after midnight.

Along with the promotion as *sostituto* came membership of the Consistorial Congregation, which selected new bishops, and of the Holy Office, the center of theological orthodoxy. A further move of residence was required, this time to a large apartment in the Apostolic Palace, adjacent to St. Peter's Basilica, that would be his residence for the next seventeen years.

Now aged forty, it seemed that Giovanni Battista Montini had come to the top of his ecclesiastical service. Only the position of cardinal secretary of state could await him. Shortly following his appointment, Pope Pius suffered a severe heart attack. His doctors insisted that the octogenarian pontiff retire to the papal country residence at Castel Gandolfo to recuperate. Pius, therefore, was not resident in Rome when the German chancellor Adolf Hitler visited Mussolini on May 3, 1938. The leader of the Nazi Party wished to forge deeper relationships with Mussolini's Fascist Party. The forced absence of the pontiff was interpreted as a rebuff to the political allies.

A month later Montini accompanied Cardinal Pacelli to the International Eucharistic Congress in the Hungarian capital, Bucharest. The country put on an impressive display of religious zeal, but all the participants were aware of the shadows gathering over Europe. On March 12 Adolf Hitler had annexed Austria, his first move to expand German control in Europe.

The prophesies of war were accurate. Although he feared that war was imminent, Pius did not live to see the outbreak of hostilities. In the early hours of February 10, 1939, he died of a second heart attack at the age of eighty-one. Montini was among those at the bedside of the pope as he breathed his last. As *sostituto*, it was his task to break the news that the See of Peter was vacant. Cardinal Pacelli immediately assumed the office of camerlengo of the church, thus assuming responsibilities that included arranging the funeral rites of the deceased pontiff and the conclave to elect his successor. He carried out his first function, leaning over the body of the pope who had breathed his last and calling out his baptismal name three times: "Achille, Achille, Achille."

CHAPTER THREE

Pius XII, the Postwar Years, and the Departure for Milan

The mood of the cardinals gathered for the conclave three weeks after the death of Pope Pius was somber. War in Europe was now seen as inevitable. Two years earlier Italy had joined a pact with Japan and Germany to break up communist activities, and Japan and China were at war. Russia was also engaged in hostilities with Japan. Of all the cardinals present, none was better placed to understand the complexity of the rapidly deteriorating situation than Cardinal Pacelli. Not only had he served as Pius's right hand for several years, but his time in Germany had given him a keen insight into national politics.

On the afternoon of March 1 sixty-three cardinals took up temporary lodgings in the Apostolic Palace to select Pius's successor. The precarious situation of Europe required a pope with refined diplomatic skills. Each day they gathered in the Sistine Chapel to vote for a new pontiff. The first ballot, held that afternoon, was inconclusive.

The election was the shortest in living memory, lasting less than two days. The two ballots of March 2 put Pacelli ahead with more than forty votes. The electors realized that Pacelli's experience was incomparable. Although he could be mercurial and temperamental, there was none to compare with his diplomatic talent. In the afternoon session, the fourth ballot of the conclave gave Pacelli the two-thirds-plus-one majority required for a valid election. It was his sixty-fourth birthday.

Shortly before 6:00 p.m. white smoke billowed from the chimney that protruded from the temporary stove in the chapel where the ballots were burned after each vote. If the ballots were inconclusive, straw was added to the fire to produce black smoke. A tall chimney rose from the stove and opened onto the roof of the chapel, alerting the people in St. Peter's Square that a pope had been chosen.

It was almost a foregone conclusion that the new pope would be Italian. The last non-Italian, the Dutch Adrian IV, had been elected in 1523 and had reigned for just seven months. Moreover, Pius XI had often hinted his hope that Pacelli would succeed him. Although not obliged to follow the indications of a dead pontiff, the cardinals realized that Pacelli had outstanding qualities. A talented linguist, an able administrator, and a man of holiness, Pacelli seemed to have all the necessary qualifications.

Taking the name Pius XII, Pacelli publicly indicated that he would continue the policies of his predecessor. By nature Pacelli was not bellicose like the deceased pontiff and sought compromise where possible. Immediately following his election he chose Cardinal Luigi Maglione, the prefect of the Sacred Congregation for the Council and former nuncio to Paris, to fill his former role as secretary of state.

Given Maglione's relative inexperience at the Secretariat of State, Montini was retained as *sostituto* and Tardini as secretary of the Curia. Montini was assigned a new apartment, still in the Apostolic Palace adjacent to St. Peter's Basilica, only a few minutes' walk from his office at the Secretariat of State. It was just thirteen years since Montini had entered the Secretariat.

The specter of the upcoming war greatly increased his workload. With his former superior now pope, Montini continued to see him along with Cardinal Maglione, on almost a daily basis. Among Montini's duties as *sostituto* was the maintenance of relations with diplomats accredited to the Holy See. Pope Pius XII, having been secretary of state for so many years, directed Montini's contacts with the diplomats, even to mediate in the Japanese, Chinese, and Russian hostilities.

Germany began its occupation of Czechoslovakia in March, and Italy laid claim to Albania a month later. In May Germany and Italy agreed on a full military alliance. Once the coronation and Easter ceremonies had been carried out, Pius concentrated all his efforts on avoiding the outbreak of war. But the political situation continued to deteriorate. Hitler's annexation of Bohemia and Moravia in March gave the pope particular concern. On August 24 Pope Pius published a document appealing for a diplomatic solution, the first draft of which was written by Montini. But the appeal was in vain, for already the Nazis and Soviets had agreed upon a nonaggression pact and were resolved to partition Poland.

War broke out on September 1, 1939, when Germany invaded Poland. Two days later Britain and France declared war on Germany. The Soviets entered Poland on September 17 and carried out the prearranged partition. Given the Vatican's geographical situation, the Holy See was anxious that Italy would not enter the war. Montini found allies among the French and British, who also wanted Italy to remain neutral. Mussolini, whose forces were unprepared for war, opted to observe rather than engage in the hostilities, at least for the time being.

In his Christmas address to the Roman Curia of that fateful year, Pope Pius XII alluded obliquely to the hostilities in Europe but avoided laying blame at the door of any single nation. He concluded by thanking the American president Franklin D. Roosevelt for sending a personal representative and his offer of assistance to end the war. Weeks later, on January 19, 1940, on the pope's express directions, Vatican Radio and the newspaper *L'Osservatore Romano* revealed the horrors of the crimes against the Poles.

The war rolled on. In May 1940 Germany invaded Holland, Belgium, Luxembourg, and France. The following month Italy declared war on Britain and France. Diplomats accredited to the Holy See could not now remain on Italian soil and were obliged to immediately seek sanctuary within the territory of Vatican City State. Residents of the Vatican were now in a quandary. Most of the employees of the Vatican were Italian and lived in Rome. Each day they had to cross the Vatican frontier and exit in the evening. The governor of Vatican City State was Cardinal Nicola Canali, who quite openly supported Mussolini's role. The clerics who worked at the Vatican, largely Italian or Roman-trained, found they had friends and family caught up in the hostilities. It was a testing time for loyalties.

From the beginning of the war, the Vatican received hundreds of thousands of enquiries as to the whereabouts of displaced people or prisoners of war. By the time the war ended in 1945 the archives contained some 2.1 million names. Most letters were addressed directly to Pope Pius searching for information about relatives. On the pope's instruction, Montini set up a group of volunteers from within the Vatican services to seek information. Often names were broadcast on Vatican Radio in the hopes that someone would have information that could then be relayed to the anxious families. Further information was gleaned through contacts in the international papal nunciatures. Montini became so engrossed in this work that he gave over several rooms in his apartment to host the workers and store the ever-increasing correspondence. He had firsthand news of the atrocities from his brother Francesco, now a doctor and a member of the resistance movement.

Pope Pius was determined to retain the Holy See's neutrality, not simply for self-preservation but so that no side could claim papal favoritism. It was a difficult endeavor as many bishops entreated the pontiff to utter some word of comfort to the victims of war that included condemnation of the perpetrators. Each day Montini received a stream of people affected by the war. He tried to unite the various nuncios in the efforts to find a solution. From Istanbul Archbishop Angelo Roncalli, later Pope John XXIII, wrote of a suggestion made by the German ambassador to Turkey, Franz Von Papen, to develop a truce. The Vatican newspaper *L'Osservatore Romano* and Vatican Radio were criticized for disseminating news that was critical of Italy's military maneuvers.

The war took a dramatic turn on December 7, 1941, with the bombing of the American fleet by the Japanese in Pearl Harbor. In response to this belligerent act, America was obliged to enter the war. In his Christmas allocution Pope Pius repeated his five-point plan for peace. For some there was a hope that America would hasten the end of the war but this was not to be. In an unexpected move in February 1942 the Holy See granted diplomatic relations with Japan. While the move infuriated President Roosevelt, the Holy See explained that it could not ignore Japanese requests, especially as some eighteen million Catholics lived in territories controlled by Japan.

By 1942 Pius realized that his condemnations of violence bore little effect. In June he protested to Marshal Henri Pétain, a member of the French war cabinet, against "the inhuman arrests and deportations of Jews from the French occupied zone to Silesia and parts of Russia."[1]

That same year, on June 27, Pope Pius formed the Institute for Religious Works. The principal purpose was to provide for the transfer of funds throughout the war-torn world and protect the funds of various religious orders and congregations.

With the political turmoil Giovanni Battista had no time to visit his parents in Brescia. He continued to send letters and spoke regularly by telephone, excusing his absence even during the annual vacation period. On a couple of occasions he invited them to travel to the Vatican and stay with him. But in the summer of 1942 Giorgio's health had deteriorated, and Giovanni Battista and his brothers kept in regular contact. By the fall, Giorgio was bedridden. Now aged eighty-two, he was frail and clearly coming toward the end of his strength. Giovanni Battista promised to visit once the Christmas rush in the Vatican had concluded.

In his Christmas address to the Roman Curia in 1942 Pope Pius appraised the "tragic face" of Europe. Although not mentioning the anti-Semitic policies of the Nazis, the pope lamented the fate of "those hundreds of thousands who, without any fault of their own, sometimes only by reason of their nationality or race, are marked down for death or progressive extinction." The German ambassador Von Ribbentrop and Mussolini were angered by the perceived abandonment of papal neutrality. Pius was aware that too forceful a denunciation might provoke a backlash against the very Jewish victims he had hoped his words would protect.

On December 26 Giovanni Battista made his customary Christmas visit to Brescia. He stayed with his parents for four days, spending time with his bedridden father before departing by train for Rome on the 29th to attend the papal Te Deum service that marked the end of the civil year at the Vatican. Accompanied to the train station by his brother Ludovico, Giovanni Battista assured him that he would return within hours if his father's health should deteriorate.

A phone call to the Vatican summoned Giovanni Battista on January 12. His father had suffered a sudden heart attack and was gone. Giovanni Battista was deeply upset by the loss of his father and his intellectual mentor. The family gathered at Brescia for the funeral, which was attended by hundreds of mourners who remembered the important part that Giorgio had played in the day-to-day life of the town, including the many politicians who honored the three terms he had served in parliament. In Rome several Masses were celebrated in memory of Giorgio Montini. At the Vatican he was recalled with particular affection for his dedication to the political role of Italian Catholics.

Personal tragedy was to strike the Montini family once more within months. On May 17 Giuditta died of a sudden heart attack. The family gathered in grief to observe the obsequies at Brescia. Following Requiem Mass and internment, the three siblings returned to Rome on May 23. Giovanni Battista insisted that his brothers stay with him at the Vatican during their period of mourning.

The political situation in early 1943 continued to deteriorate. Mussolini and Hitler engaged in regular public spats. The Grand Council, the ruling fascist body, had not met since December 1939, just months following the outbreak of the war. As *sostituto* Giovanni Battista followed the Italian situation on behalf of the pope and reported on developments regularly. Having served as secretary through most of the previous decade, Pius had an uncommon knowledge of the workings of the Secretariat of State. He charged Montini to investigate the future of post-fascist Italy and prepare a dossier. Meanwhile, several diplomats who had taken refuge in the Vatican urged Giovanni Battista to influence Pius to take a more stringent line with the belligerents. As news spread from Germany about the horrors of the work camps, diplomats pleaded with Pius to condemn the German treatment of minorities in the clearest terms.

Despite the precarious political situation at the Vatican, the pope continued his task as universal pastor, publishing a seminal document on the church, *Mystici Corporis*, on June 29, 1943. The encyclical considered developments in ecclesiology. The publication was overshadowed on July 19, however, as Rome was bombed. Some five hundred American planes flew over the city intent on bombing the railway lines but most missed their targets. As 1,168 tons of explosives fell on the working-class area of San Lorenzo, up to three thousand citizens were maimed and killed. It was the first of a series of bombing campaigns over the Eternal City.

As the bombs began to fall, Giovanni Battista was attending a meeting with Harold Tittman, American assistant to Myron Taylor, the personal representative of President Franklin Roosevelt, at his residence in the Palazzo Santa Marta. He returned to the Secretariat of State to inform the pope, who immediately summoned a car to the area where the bombs had fallen in order to comfort the injured and bereaved. For almost three hours they walked among the wounded and visited the Basilica of San Lorenzo, which had been hit and whose roof had collapsed.

The bombing of July 19 was a presage of what was to come. A second bombing was carried out on August 13. The following day Pius appealed that Rome should be declared an open city (meaning the city had abandoned its fortifications and defense). Yet, less than a month later, German troops entered Rome. Italy had capitulated to the Allies on September 8, 1943. Two days later Nazi troops established their presence in the city. Cardinal Maglione, the secretary of state, realized that soon the Vatican, despite its neutrality, could be compromised.

On September 14, Allied ambassadors and diplomats who had taken refuge in the Vatican agreed to Maglione's suggestion that all papers and documents that might prove useful to the Nazis should be destroyed in case of invasion. The British began the destruction of the archives, and the Americans finished destroying the files on September 23. On this date Mussolini started a new government based in the Italian town of Salo. Amid the uncertainty of the times the Holy See refused to recognize the legitimacy of the establishment of an interim government.

On November 5, 1943, the Vatican was bombed. There was little damage and nobody was killed, but it greatly unnerved Pope Pius. Already three months earlier, on August 4, Cardinal Maglione had confided in the cardinals resident in Rome that the Italian authorities believed Hitler intended to invade the Vatican and kidnap the pope. Informed of the plot, Pius moved from his official quarters to a smaller apartment in the Apostolic Palace. He prepared a document of abdication in the event that he was kidnapped and unable to carry out his duties.

German troops in Italy oversaw the exportation of thousands of Jews. Pius protested through diplomatic channels, but also sheltered several thousand Jews both at the Vatican and in the papal country residence, Castel Gandolfo, in the Alban Hills. In addition clandestine help was given by many convents, monasteries, and religious houses.

In September 1943, the Nazi lieutenant colonel Herbert Kappler, on orders from Berlin, demanded the payment of sixty kilos of gold by the Jewish community. When the Jews petitioned Pope Pius to help raise the required gold, the pontiff promised the necessary loan, although it was not required as the Jews managed to produce the gold from their own resources. On October 16 Nazi troops rounded up 1,015 Jews who inhabited the area around the synagogue in the old Jewish Ghetto. Although the "ransom" demanded by Berlin had been raised, the deportation went ahead. Informed of the atrocity, Pius could do little more than lament their fate. The German Gestapo appeared unstoppable.

Montini and Tardini continued to seek a solution to the deluge of human misery. The network that helped find people missing in the war continued to receive new staff to deal with the mounting number of refugees. Meanwhile the Holy See had to prepare to deal with the postwar Italian government. Montini was well placed to offer counsel as he knew so many young professionals and politicians from his days as chaplain of FUCI.

On March 24, 1944, 335 people were rounded up by German soldiers and brought to the Ardeatine Caves on the outskirts of Rome. Blindfolded and with their hands tied behind their backs, they were machine-gunned to death in reprisal for the assassination of German soldiers some days earlier. Food rationing and fuel restrictions had made life in Rome difficult, but the shooting at the caves quelled any further hints of insurrection against the Germans.

The beginning of the end of the war came quickly. Mussolini was captured and executed by Italian partisans on April 28, 1945. Two days later Hitler committed suicide in a bunker in Berlin. Hostilities in Italy ceased on May 2. Within a short period of time, the political scene changed dramatically. On June 4 the Allies liberated the city. The pope was hailed for his role in liberating Rome, although in reality he had played no part in the military maneuvers.

The war was still not entirely over, however, for Japan remained to surrender. Hostilities were to continue in the East and finally came to an end with the horrific bombing of Hiroshima and Nagasaki in August. The two bombings, ordered by US President Harry S. Truman, were the only nuclear devices deployed in the war.

As peace was established, diplomats who had taken refuge in the Vatican were able to leave and return home. Yet while Rome was free and France was liberated that same month, Pope Pius looked anxiously at communist Russia and the Eastern bloc countries. The Nazi regime had been defeated by the Allies but the Soviet threat of atheistic communism remained. The Cold War was soon to begin.

With the end of the war came freedom of movement. Pope Pius convoked his first consistory to create thirty-two cardinals on February 18, 1946. This brought the number to the traditional limit of seventy members. Only four of the new cardinals were Italian, the rest distributed among Argentina, Canada, Brazil, Germany, China, Mozambique, England, Chile, France, Poland, Hungary, Armenia, Australia, Germany, Spain, Holland, Peru, and the United States. A number of the new cardinals had been vociferous opponents of Nazism.

In postwar Italy the population elected a new government. King Victor Emmanuel III abdicated on May 4, 1946. The kingdom of Italy was abolished, the Royal House of Savoy was exiled, and a republic was established. On June 2, the first free elections since 1924 were held. The result was to form a Constituent Assembly of 556 deputies who were charged to draft the constitution for a new republic. As Italy elected a new government the pope indicated his preference for one elected by the people. While the church had long expressed caution for democracy, Pius hoped to foster the election of anti-fascists and keep communists, the largest political party in Western Europe, from power.

Montini favored the Christian Democrats, led by Alcide De Gasperi, who became prime minister in 1945. De Gasperi obtained funds for Italy from the American-inspired Marshall Plan, designed to assist Europe rebuild itself. De Gasperi was a proponent of NATO and worked for the foundation of the European Union. By the terms of the Lateran Treaty of 1929, the Holy See had to maintain strict impartiality and could not interfere in national affairs. Among the collateral effects of the Second World War were the close ties forged between the United States and Europe. The war had shaken old alliances. Although excluded from the peace negotiations following the cessation of the war, the Holy See still had a role to play.

Tardini continued to be in charge of external relations while Montini governed internal matters. Yet their roles overlapped, often to the annoyance of Tardini. Increasingly, Montini became the conduit between the pope and the rest of the world. With Cardinal Maglione's death in 1944, Pius decided not to appoint a new secretary of state and informally assumed the role himself. In this capacity the pope received Montini early each morning for a briefing. Mornings and afternoons were taken up with courtesy calls from visitors who were obliged to wait for hours to have a short audience with Montini.

The range of visitors was broad. The archbishop of Canterbury made overtures to the Holy See, and the Anglican bishop Stephen Neill of the newly founded World Council of Churches also met with the *sostituto*. On June 6, 1949, Montini received Br. Roger Schutz and Max Thurian, who had together founded an ecumenical monastery in Switzerland, and Montini presented the two to Pope Pius the following day. Although Cardinal Ottaviani of the Holy Office disapproved of such meetings, there was little he could do to prevent them. Pius saw such encounters as the presage to the full union of Christians under the leadership of the Bishop of Rome.

In 1948 Ottaviani and Cardinal Ernesto Ruffini of Palermo in Sicily proposed that the pope host an ecumenical council at the Vatican. The previous council (now known as the First Vatican Council) had been suspended by Pope Pius IX on October 20, 1870, when the bishops hastily left Rome at the outbreak of the Franco-Prussian War. Pope Pius was not convinced that the time was ripe for a council. Already the calendar was full and the forthcoming jubilee year of 1950 was to dominate Rome and the Catholic world. Initiated by Pope Boniface VIII in 1300, the "holy years" took place every quarter of a century. The forthcoming jubilee would mark 1,950 years since the traditional date for the birth of Christ. The idea of a council was therefore postponed. Pius was now seventy-four and had little appetite to undertake such a major event.

Charged with the preparation of the jubilee year, Montini formed a committee under the direction of his friend Monsignor Sergio Pignedoli. The Italian civil authorities saw the jubilee as an opportunity to both showcase the new postwar government and promote Rome as the capital of both the ancient and modern world. The year-long celebration was an opportunity to demonstrate the central role of the papacy. Some three million pilgrims undertook the journey to Rome to pray at the tombs of St. Peter and St. Paul. There were colorful processions, youth jamborees, canonization ceremonies, prayer vigils, and elaborate Masses.

The publication that year of the encyclical *Humani Generis* on developments in modern theology was an exercise of Pius's lofty view of the papacy as an arbitrator of the faith. In the document Pius warned the bishops to resist theological trends that he believed were dangerous, although he made some novel moves in the area of evolution and creationism. While he recognized the convincing arguments for evolution, he argued that only God could create and instill a soul in each human.

On the feast of All Saints, November 1, 1950, Pius infallibly defined the doctrine of the assumption of Mary into heaven. This was the first time the act of infallibility had been invoked since its definition at the First Vatican Council seventy years earlier. There had been little appetite for such a decree. The New Testament was silent on the end of Mary's life. Pius decreed that Mary had been assumed, body and soul, to paradise, although he stopped short of saying that this had followed after her death. The declaration greatly boosted popular devotion to the Blessed Virgin. The invocation of infallibility did much to raise the spiritual authority of the papacy in the eyes of Catholics, with few publicly dissenting voices.

As the year drew to a close, Montini engaged in the preparatory meetings for the Congress of the Laity, which was to have its first meeting a year later. Montini showed his interest in what was soon to be called the Apostolate of the Laity. His vision was strictly hierarchical, with clergy at the top of a pyramid whose broad base was the laity. This was the predominant view of clerics who served in the Holy See.

Swollen audiences distracted Pope Pius from the more routine work of the Secretariat, greatly increasing Montini's workload. The opening months of 1951 allowed the pope and Curia to return to a more normal pace. As Pius continued to fulfill the role of secretary of state he came to rely increasingly on Tardini and Montini for assistance. Documents, discourses, sermons, and encyclicals had to be prepared by a relatively small staff.

On June 2, 1951, the pope issued the encyclical *Evangelii Praecones* on the role of Catholic missionaries. While he deplored persecutions in some territories such as China, he welcomed the contribution that many cultures made to Christianity. At the end of his summer vacation in Castel Gandolfo Pius issued another encyclical, *Ingruentium Malorum*, on the recitation of the rosary. In addition, the pontiff received audiences and gave allocutions to pilgrims and congresses from all over the world. There was little that escaped Pius's interest. His photographic mind allowed him to memorize speeches rapidly and master a number of languages.

In early October the First International Congress on the Apostolate of the Laity took place. The pope addressed the delegates at the end of the congress on October 14, encouraging the formation of other branches throughout the world.

On January 12, 1953, Pope Pius held the second and last consistory of his pontificate, during which he created twenty-four cardinals, ten of whom were Italian. Neither Montini nor Tardini's names were on the list. Given that so long had elapsed since the first consistory, it was evident that Montini would not be named a cardinal during Pius's pontificate. This also ruled him out as a possible successor, for all popes in recent centuries had been cardinals prior to election.

Writing after the death of Pope Pius, in a short biography of the deceased pope, Tardini claimed that both men had been offered the cardinal's hat by Pius but that each had refused it in order to remain at the aging pontiff's side. Pius obliquely thanked them for their refusal during his address to the new cardinals on January 12, 1953. Pius knew that Montini would be *papabile*, but by not creating him a cardinal, or appointing him to a diocese, he knew that Montini would not be his immediate successor.

With failing health, Pius became evermore dependent on his two collaborators and needed his trusted delegates. Pius had a curious relationship with the Curia. Having been in charge for years under Pius XI, Pacelli grew increasingly remote. He funneled his commands through his secretaries. He simply wanted people who would obediently carry out his orders and avoid any display of initiative.

Among the issues that dominated the pope's attention was the priest workers. In 1944 a number of missions were set up in Paris that allowed priests to work in factories for some hours each day. The pioneer of the movement was Fr. Jacques Loew, a Dominican who joined dock workers in Marseilles in 1941. The idea was to allow the priests to work closely with people so that they could both know their daily problems and be readily available to them. By earning their own wage, it also freed them from dependence on a parish. Further missions were set up in Lyons and Marseilles. Among the first witnesses to the enterprise was a young Fr. Karol Wojtyla, who was initially impressed by the new way of approaching workers, many of whom had lapsed from the Catholic faith.

The apostolic nuncio in Paris, Archbishop Angelo Roncalli, had reservations about the movement but agreed not to oppose the movement if it was on a trial basis. Montini followed the developments from Rome. The experiment did not progress smoothly and the laity, priests, and bishops were divided on its merits. Several denounced developments to the Vatican. "Of every two Frenchmen," Montini later observed to his friend Jean Guitton, "there is always one ready to pack his bags and come to Rome to denounce the other."[2]

In late 1953 Pope Pius decided to suppress the worker priest enterprise. He delayed putting his provisions into action before Christmas, however, and in late January Pius became ill. The cause of his sickness was not made public but for several months he curtailed his audiences and was attended only by his medical and household staff. During this period his housekeeper, the Bavarian nun, Sr. Pascalina Lehnert, was in virtual control of access to the elderly pope. It was the beginning of a decline that lasted until his death four years later.

On August 30, 1954, the seventy-four-year-old archbishop of Milan, Cardinal Ildefonso Schuster, died. Three days later Cardinal Angelo Roncalli, the recently appointed patriarch of Venice, celebrated Requiem Mass in Milan's Duomo. Schuster's death presented Pius with an important decision. With a population of 3.5 million, a thousand churches served by two-and-a-half thousand priests, Milan was Italy's largest and most prestigious diocese. Schuster had been a Benedictine monk and abbot at the Roman Basilica of St. Paul Outside-the-Walls prior to his appointment to Milan in 1929. Religious practice had declined dramatically in the city, and the peripheries were filled with factories served by thousands of migrants from southern Italy. The challenge was to find a pastorally minded bishop with honed experience in administration.

Having considered the vacancy carefully, Pius decided that Montini should leave his side and go to Milan. Montini was astonished when he received the news. It was certainly an elevation but not one that he had expected. By now Montini had been at the Vatican for some thirty-four years and had perhaps reasonably presumed that he would end his life in service of the Holy See.

Montini had enemies. His proximity to the pope had roused jealousy among several senior curial members. Some resented his apparent openness to new methods of theology. While Pius informed Montini privately of his intentions in mid-October, the announcement was made on November 3, so that it could be made public the following day, the feast of the celebrated seventeenth-century archbishop of Milan, St. Charles Borromeo. Curiously, the news leaked and published in the French daily, *Le Monde*, on October 22.

On December 12, St. Peter's Basilica was thronged with Brescians and Milanese along with the friends Montini had made over three decades in Rome. The consecration ceremony for his elevation as archbishop was to have been presided over by the pope. Due to the pontiff's illness, the Pontifical High Mass was celebrated by Cardinal Eugène Tisserant, dean of the Sacred College of Cardinals. A reception was held in the Apostolic Palace following the ceremony to bid farewell to the erstwhile number two in the Secretariat of State. A series of farewell receptions were held around Rome during the days prior to Christmas.

While the new archbishop's belongings and furniture were dispatched to Milan, Montini went home to visit his family for the Christmas break. The date of his formal arrival in Milan was January 5, 1955. Having overnighted in the Lombard city of Lodi, Montini was collected by car and entered his new diocese at Melegano, some eight miles outside Milan. Crossing the boundary, he requested the driver to stop. Alighting from the car and with head uncovered, he knelt to kiss the rain-soaked ground of his new diocese. He then proceeded to the official residence beside the great Gothic cathedral of Milan.

Rain continued to pour the following day, January 6, the feast of the Epiphany. Vested in a purple silk *cappa magna* and *galero*, the new archbishop drove through the crowds in an open-top car to the cathedral, where he celebrated Mass. In his inaugural sermon, Archbishop Montini pledged his fidelity to serving the complex and enormous diocese. The crowds were pleased that not only had they a fellow Lombard as their new pastor but that he had come, in the words of Pius XII, "as a personal gift."

Although not a cardinal, it was inevitable that the next pope would confer upon Milan the traditional red hat. Montini had little interest in personal honors. With no hesitation he threw himself into the complex world of Milan. At the first gathering of clergy in Milan he confessed that he had much to learn from their wisdom and experience.

From the beginning he established a routine, rising early to celebrate morning Mass, attending to correspondence and receiving visitors in audience. After a frugal lunch he continued to work at his desk until the early evening. Some afternoons and evenings he visited factories, donning a steel hat in place of his biretta, or schools and hospitals. Postwar Italy was enjoying an economic boom based largely in the north of Italy and centered around the metropolis of Milan. Montini also continued to keep up his interest in international affairs. Each morning the French newspaper *Le Figaro* and *The New York Times* were delivered to his office. Given the contacts he had made while at the Vatican he also maintained a considerable correspondence.

Even for the fastidious Montini, the pace proved too much and within three months of his arrival the new bishop suffered a physical breakdown. On medical advice he retired to the seminary for a period of several weeks of total rest, which required his absence from the ceremonies of Holy Week and his first Easter in Milan. He returned to the diocese on April 12, having promised his doctor that he would reduce his workload. Following a further period of rest during the summer, the new archbishop began a series of pastoral visits of all 950 parishes of the archdiocese, beginning with the parish of the cathedral on September 8.

From the outset Montini was aware of the need to address the social and cultural problems of the city. Seeing his role as a bridge-builder he hosted meetings of artists, politicians, industrialists, and members of trade unions. Given his love of art and architecture, he was also an assiduous builder of churches. Old chapels that had been closed for decades were renovated. Within months of his arrival, Montini began a huge program of church building, eventually adding over one hundred new churches throughout the diocese and overseeing their artistic and liturgical furnishings.

In his new thirty-one-year-old private secretary, Don Pasquale Macchi, Montini found a dedicated assistant. A native of nearby Varese, Macchi had been ordained nine years earlier and had an encyclopedic knowledge of the vast diocese. Macchi shared Montini's passion for art and introduced his superior to contemporary Milanese artists.

Having overcome the initial shock of life outside the Vatican, Montini soon found his stride. Accustomed to serving the pope, he was now the final arbiter in his own diocese. He moved into the role of pastoral bishop slowly, supporting the clergy of the diocese and visiting the parishes. While the majority of churches were near the historical center of Milan, Montini traveled by car to even the remotest rural areas and on occasion even traveled by donkey.

Montini brought the talents honed in service of the Holy See to Milan. Cardinal Schuster had been an undeniably holy pastor but he had left the diocese with severe financial difficulties and a poor administration. Montini spent the first eighteen months of his period in office tackling the historical problems of the diocese. Although a professional consultancy firm had advised on a radical restructuring of the diocese, Montini decided against implementing it, preferring to preserve the clerical status quo and also in order to avoid offending the elderly clergy. Both the resources and challenges of the diocese were enormous. The population at the time of Montini's arrival in Milan numbered three million and was served by 2,350 priests, 1,025 religious brothers, 14,519 religious sisters, and 1,073 consecrated members of secular institutes.

The archbishop continued to make occasional visits to Rome, and through correspondence with various ecclesiastics remained well informed regarding the Vatican, which continued to see a rapid decline in the pope's health. By late 1956 close observers knew that the pontificate would soon come to an end.

In the same year, Archbishop Montini decided to hold a mission for the city. The idea of such an outreach had been tried in various dioceses both in Italy and Europe. Given that Milan was the largest diocese on the continent, the challenge was all the greater. With the assistance of his auxiliary bishop, Sergio Pignedoli, Montini decided to launch a mission commencing in 1957. Undertaking the vast enterprise were 1,288 preachers, including 2 cardinals and 24 bishops. Five thousand banners hung from buildings. One priest organized a series of retreats for 70 fashion models while other retreats accommodated the members of the city's stock market. Other spiritual events took place day and night for the thousands of southern Italians who had flocked to Milan in search of work in postwar Italy. "Knock on everybody's door," counseled Montini prudently, "but don't knock the door down!"

The mission, which began in Advent 1957, was largely clerical. The program was designed for clergy to preach to laypeople. The apostolate of the laity was little understood. The mission, for all its success, reflected a largely passive laity guided by the clergy. To conclude the mission Pope Pius delivered a radio message that was broadcast from the Vatican on national radio.

During the year following the mission, Montini instituted the Office of Studies, which correlated the achievements of the enterprise and addressed issues that had arisen during its course.

During the summer of 1958 Pope Pius's health deteriorated further. After several weeks of being confined to bed, the eighty-two-year-old pontiff died at Castel Gandolfo on October 9. As the nineteen-year pontificate came to a close most realized it was also the end of an era. The pope's body was brought in cortege to Rome, pausing at St. John Lateran en route. Enormous crowds lined the streets and hundreds of thousands filed into St. Peter's Basilica to pay their final respects.

Following the funeral rites, those remaining cardinals not yet present were summoned to Rome to begin the process of electing a new pope. No non-Italian had been elected since Adrian VI (1523), and the presumption was that the new pope would be Italian.

CHAPTER FOUR

John XXIII, the Council, and the Election of John Baptist

The conclave of fifty-one cardinal electors was held in the Sistine Chapel between October 25 and 28, 1958. The new pope needed thirty-five votes to secure election. The emergence of the seventy-seven-year-old Cardinal Angelo Roncalli, patriarch of Venice, was a surprise. It indicated that after the two-decade pontificate of Pius XII the cardinals judged that a shorter reign would be preferable.

Taking the name John XXIII, the new pope set about addressing what he saw as an injustice to his friend Montini. Among his first acts, just two weeks after his coronation, John announced a consistory to create new cardinals. First among the twenty-three names on the list was that of Giovanni Battista Montini.

The friendship between the two men stretched back thirty years. Roncalli was a self-confessed gossip, and the papal court was for him a constant source of fascination. Although he had spent most of his life outside Rome as a diplomat, he corresponded regularly with Montini, and when passing through Rome he always made a point of calling upon Montini and dining with him. Roncalli's decision to create Montini a cardinal ensured that Montini would attend the conclave following Pope John's death. Pius XII had internationalized the College of Cardinals by creating new members from around the globe, more than any other pope had done. The expanded number of cardinals reflected the growing number of Catholics worldwide, especially in Latin America and sub-Saharan Africa.

During a liturgical celebration to mark the feast of the Conversion of St. Paul on January 25, 1959, Pope John XXIII announced to the assembled cardinals his decision to hold an ecumenical council. The idea had come to him just a few days after his election. The pope's proposal was received with complete silence by the College of Cardinals. Writing in his diary that night, the normally complacent John expressed his irritation at their lack of enthusiasm.

Montini was among those who hesitated before the idea of a council. The last such gathering at the Vatican in 1870 had broken up in disarray due to the political situation in Italy, and there were few who saw any need for a council. Moreover, John was now seventy-eight and several cardinals doubted whether he would have the stamina required to convene and conclude a full council.

For friendship's sake and with a sense of fidelity to the papal office, Montini supported his old friend's proposal. Whatever doubts he harbored about the wisdom of the endeavor, the archbishop of Milan assured the pope of his unreserved loyal support. Montini encouraged the press to take an interest in the council, and he wrote several articles on the upcoming event. These gave rise to the establishment of the monthly newspaper *Diocese of Milan*, later known as *Terra Ambrosiana*. Each year in November he hosted a meeting for journalists during which he inevitably recalled his father's profession and his own interest in writing.

The style of Montini's sermons and addresses was always paternalistic. Like most of his episcopal colleagues in Italy, he treated the people of his diocese as passive observers. Their task was to listen to the teachings of the bishop and learn from his wisdom. The people were not expected to offer advice and, much less, oppose whatever the bishops proposed. Within a few years the deliberations of the Second Vatican Council altered the traditional pattern irrevocably.

While Montini's public utterances about the council were positive, he continued to have doubts about its merits. From his friends in Rome he discovered that many in the Roman Curia were vehemently opposed, considering the timing unsuitable. They pragmatically accepted that as Pope John wanted the council it would be best for the Curia to set the agenda.

Montini, through the years of private correspondence, knew that John was critical of the way several members of the Curia worked. John wished to try a gentle reform. Montini welcomed the opportunity to make the central government offices more effective. Having spent three decades at the Vatican, he was well aware of the machinations that made the papacy resemble a medieval court. The last decade of Pacelli's pontificate in particular had been marked with stifling inertia.

Montini heard from former colleagues that the pope had taken to making surprise visits to see Vatican employees at work. As he strolled along the corridors, word soon went round to keep the desks tidy in case the pontiff arrived unannounced.

Montini was in favor of devolving issues that did not need to be submitted to Rome, preferring instead that they be resolved at the local level. He shared John's vision that a council could foster better unity among Christians. But even John saw ecumenism in terms of Protestants and other heretics returning to the Catholic fold. Such reunion was to prove elusive, however, even half a century following the end of the council.

In 1960 Montini took an uncharacteristically long vacation, spending a month in the United States and Brazil. He visited thirteen cities and joined President Dwight Eisenhower at the University of Notre Dame in Indiana, where both received honorary doctorates. He impressed his American hosts with his gentle demeanor and lack of formality, traveling in a simple black suit and black fedora hat.

To the task of administering the Diocese of Milan was added another responsibility when, in November 1961, Montini was appointed to the Central Preparatory Committee of the council that had been under the chairmanship of Cardinal Tardini since the previous May. Tardini had died of a massive heart attack on July 30 at the Villa Nazareth, the orphanage he had founded for boys in 1946. Two weeks later, on August 12, John appointed his contemporary Ameleto Cicognani as secretary of state, governor of Vatican City State, and president of the Administration of the Patrimony of the Apostolic See. Cicognani was better disposed to the council than Tardini, and he applied his skills to carrying the preparations forward. Now in the high summer there was little that could be done until the traditional vacation period for Romans had ended. Yet John was in a hurry and continued to press for progress.

For Montini, membership on the committee required regular visits to Rome and added to the already considerable amount of documentation through which he had to wade. In digesting the documents, Montini was assisted by a

Milanese theologian, Monsignor Carlo Colombo, later an auxiliary bishop of Milan.

The Central Preparatory Committee began to gather views from bishops throughout the world. The council would be primarily a gathering of bishops, although John later added a number of nonvoting observers. Since only a small number of bishops were noted for their theological prowess, many employed the assistance of professional theologians, as *periti*, or experts. Non-Catholic leaders were also invited as observers.

The early months of 1962 were almost entirely taken up with preparations for the council, which was due to begin in October. Seventy-two schema, or draft documents, had been composed by the preparatory commission on a variety of issues.

On March 19, 1962, John held his fifth and final consistory at which ten cardinals were created. Among them was the Belgian Leo Jozef Suenens, whom he had appointed archbishop of Mechelen-Brussels the previous November. The pope received Suenens shortly after the consistory in a private meeting. The new cardinal took Pope John by surprise by his severe critique of the preparations for the council, including accusations of incompetence at various levels within the Curia.

Suenens argued that the amount of work already submitted would effectively drown efforts at renewal. John listened carefully and agreed with Suenens. The Belgian warned him that the council could do more harm than good by building up public expectations that were unlikely to be fulfilled. The pope asked Suenens to summarize the meeting in a few points and send them to him in the form of a memo. Before the archbishop left, John suggested that Suenens speak with Montini and the cardinal of Lille, Achille Liénart. By the end of April Suenens wrote to the pope with a summary of what he believed was needed.

Suenens recommended reducing the schema and referring several issues to the Commission for the Revision of Canon Law or permanent postconciliar commissions rather than take up time on the council floor. Suenens hinted that the Curia wanted to filibuster and concluded with the suggestion that greater power be given to local episcopal conferences to neutralize the Curia. John was heartened by Suenens's suggestions and ordered their implementation. The bishops and theologians had been consulted, and their views and suggestions were incorporated into the documents.

Roncalli had not kept abreast with contemporary theology, although he had widely read the Greek and Latin fathers. During his pontificate he had little time to read emerging theologians and was therefore unable to follow the developments of ecumenical scholarship. As he worked through the *schemae* John found himself in agreement with Suenens's suggestions. The drafts, now preserved in the papal archives, show pencil marks crossing out passages and marginal notes requesting that ghost writers be more positive in their proposals.

Pope John realized that many cardinals and bishops were less than well disposed to the council. His way of overcoming this imbalance was to ask bishops he knew personally and nuncios throughout the world to recommend theologians and experts whom he appointed to the commissions. He understood that the council needed a broader appeal than the Catholic Church. On July 20, invitations were sent to various Protestant and Orthodox bodies, inviting them to send observers to the council.

In the early summer, John began to feel unwell. He rapidly lost weight and felt listless. In May he suffered a hemorrhage and on medical advice cancelled a number of audiences. Hoping that the annual vacation at Castel Gandolfo would restore his energy, he mentioned his discomfort during his fortnightly visits with his doctor. There seemed little cause for alarm, as initially it was thought that the pain might be caused by a stomach ulcer. John pushed on with his preparations for the council, publishing a list with the names of ten heads of commissions, along with regulations governing the procedures.

Despite medication, the discomfort continued and on September 23, 1962, John underwent an X-ray at the Vatican. The diagnosis confirmed an advanced stomach tumor. Two of his siblings had died with similar ailments so John knew what to expect. He forbade the news to be made public as he did not want his illness to interfere with the preparation of the impending council. "At least," he confided to his secretary, Monsignor Capovilla, "let us pray that I may launch the ship. Another can guide it to port."[1]

With the opening date set on October 11, 1962, there was little time to compose an agenda and circulate it to all the bishops of the world. Questionnaires, however, were sent out for the bishops to make their own proposals. The role of bishops was suggested as a topic, as was a reform of the liturgy. Most bishops believed with Pope John that the council would be completed within a few months and that they could return to their dioceses. If all went to plan, the council would be over by Christmas with a reaffirmation of the glories of the Catholic faith. Not all relished the idea of spending a long period in Rome.

The council opened on the morning of October 11, 1963, with a solemn pontifical High Mass presided over by Pope John. After forty-four intensive months of preparation, the council was to begin with 2,778 bishops, cardinals, and patriarchs in attendance. Under a brilliant blue sky, the pope was carried in procession from the Apostolic Palace through St. Peter's Square into the basilica. The colorful parade lasted an hour and a quarter. Vested in a white and gold silk jeweled miter and cope, the elderly John dispensed blessings to the enormous crowd.

In his sermon, Pope John urged the assembled bishops to bring the joy of the Gospel message to the modern world. In particular he denounced the "prophets of doom" who saw threats to the Catholic faith at every turn and were afraid of modern times. Recalling his January 25, 1959, announcement of the council, he observed it was "as though some ray of supernatural light had entered the minds of all present. It was reflected in their faces, it shone from their eyes."[2] Many of the cardinals wryly realized the pope had modified his recollection of the event.

That evening a procession of Romans and visitors poured into St. Peter's Square to thank the pontiff for convening the council. Montini walked from his lodgings in the Casa Santa Marta to the side of St. Peter's Basilica to watch the extraordinary spectacle. Despite the fatigue of the long day, Pope John, who had already retired for the night, came to the window of his study. He thanked the people for their show of affection:

> Dear children, I hear your voices. Mine is just one voice, but it gathers the voices of the whole world. Here the world is represented. One could even say that the moon hastened to be present to see the event, which even St. Peter's, in four centuries, has never seen. I am nobody, but I am a brother who speaks to you and I have become a father through the Lord's will.
>
> When you return home, you will find children. Give a caress to your children and say to them, "This is the caress

of the pope." You will find some tears to dry, so say a kind word—"the pope is with us, especially in times of bitter sadness."[3]

John's health continued to deteriorate through the end of the year. By early 1963 it was clear that he was dying. His continued loss of weight and energy was visible to all. He limited his public appearances but encouraged preparations for the next council session, which was due to take place in the fall. Although he knew his successor would not be bound to continue the council, he fervently hoped that it would be brought to a successful conclusion within the year. John was also clearly aware that many of the council fathers were ill disposed to his openness and were determined to finish the business as soon as possible. But all of that would depend on his successor.

Just days before Pope John died in the papal apartment of the Apostolic Palace, the pontiff's family were ushered in to say their farewells. They had traveled by plane from Milan, accompanied by Cardinal Montini. After a painful struggle, John died in the evening of Pentecost Sunday, June 3, at 7:49 p.m. "My bags are packed," he murmured shortly before his passing.

For several months people had known of John's imminent demise. Tens of thousands gathered each day in the piazza to accompany him with their prayers and good wishes. He was universally mourned by Catholics and non-Catholics alike for his optimism, piety, and good humor. Montini had lost a good friend, a patron, and the faithful correspondent of three decades.

As Rome prepared for John's obsequies, the eighty-two eligible cardinals began to consider the succession. The papacy is the oldest surviving nonhereditary monarchy in the world. Once elected supreme pontiff, the pope has absolute power. As none but a handful of pontiffs had abdicated in its two-millennia history, the cardinals needed to choose their candidate carefully. While a pope might abdicate, there was no provision in law for deposing a pope unwilling to leave office.

Several determining factors governed the election. Given that the council was in session, the new pope would have the freedom to continue or close the proceedings. Accordingly, they needed a candidate that corresponded with their wishes. The fate of the Second Vatican Council—and John's legacy—hung in the balance.

Since the College of Cardinals had been internationalized, the possibility of electing the first non-Italian pope since 1523 had to be considered. From the outset, however, the presumption was that the next pope would be chosen from one of the twenty-nine cardinals present, despite the globalization of the College initiated by Pope Pius XII.

The last of the cardinals arrived in Rome by mid-June and quietly began to inform themselves about each other. No cardinal is permitted to canvass for his own election. Montini was one of the last to reach Rome, arriving by plane from Milan on the evening of June 16. His was a difficult position to be in, as his name was widely mentioned among the prominent Italian candidates. He did not want to appear as a "kingmaker," but if he refused to play the role it indicated that he was aware and willing to have his name put forward as a candidate. Having deposited his luggage at the Sisters of the Bambino Gesù, he prudently left the city for a few days to spend time with his friend Emilio Bonomelli, the director of the papal villa of Castel Gandolfo.

The conclave began on the afternoon of June 19. Makeshift cubicles had been erected in the Apostolic Palace for the eighty participants. Cardinal József Mindszenty of Hungary had been prohibited by the government to travel, while Cardinal Carlo María de la Torre was too ill to attend. Of the cardinals who entered the Sistine Chapel to vote, eight had been created by Pope Pius XI, twenty-seven by Pope Pius XII, while the remainder had been elevated by Pope John.

The Sistine Chapel, constructed by Pope Sixtus IV, had been the venue for most of the conclaves since its construction five centuries earlier. Many of the most celebrated artists of the Renaissance, Ghirlandaio, Perugino, and Botticelli, had decorated the walls with magnificent frescos. Dominating the chapel was the creation of the world on the vault and the last judgment above the High Altar, the work of Michelangelo.

Having sung the ninth-century Latin hymn *Veni Creator Spiritus* invoking the aid of the Holy Spirit, the scarlet-clad cardinals took an oath on the Book of the Gospels to choose the best candidate according to their conscience and to preserve the confidentiality of the proceedings. Despite the oath, several cardinals later recounted snippets of the proceedings, allowing historians to surmise the general thrust of the process.

Two ballots took place on the first afternoon, while four were scheduled for each successive day. Around the walls of the chapel were arranged chairs and desks above which stood a canopy. All would be lowered upon the election, apart from that above the newly elected pontiff. Ballot papers were distributed to each cardinal with the Latin text *Eligo in Summum Pontificem* (I elect as Supreme Pontiff) with space where the name of the candidate could be inserted. Each cardinal was expected to disguise his handwriting. The cardinals approached the altar and placed their ballot on a gilt paten before tipping it into a chalice. At the end of each session three cardinal scrutineers counted the votes.

The afternoon ballots of the first session proved inconclusive but indicated the mind of the majority of cardinals. Of the Italians, the most likely to attain a majority were Giacomo Lecaro of Bologna, Giuseppe Siri of Genoa, and Montini of Milan. By the fourth ballot of the second day it was clear that Montini was close to gaining the majority of the votes, two-thirds plus one. One cardinal, Gustavo Testa, had loudly protested in the chapel against the cardinals who sought to block Montini's election. As the balloting concluded for the day the cardinals retired for a light evening meal. The election was imminent. When supper was finished Montini retired to his cell. His secretary, Don Pasquale Macchi, recorded that he remained awake most of the night.

By morning all was decided. During the night hours several cardinals gathered to discuss in small groups the swelling consensus for Montini. They realized the importance of a swift result. A hung conclave would send signals of division, and thus place the council in jeopardy, so the remaining undecided cardinals swung behind Montini's candidacy. As the scrutineers called out the names following the first ballot the next morning, Montini's name rang out repeatedly. Several cardinals kept a tally. As soon as the majority had been reached, fifty-four plus one, applause broke out. A pope had been elected. Their task was done.

Although protocol demanded that the remaining ballots be called out, Montini was the choice of the majority of the cardinals. All that remained was the formal proposition by the cardinal dean who approached the candidate. *Acceptasne electionem de te canonice factam in Summum Pontificem?* "Do you accept your canonical election as Supreme Pontiff?" Montini nodded and gave his acceptance, *Accepto*. The dean continued, *Quo nomine quis vocari?* "By what name will you be called?" *Vocabor Paulus.* "I will be called Paul."

The tradition of changing one's name upon election dated to the sixth century when the priest Mercury was selected by the clergy and people of Rome. Not desiring to retain the name of a Roman pagan god, the presbyter changed his name to John. The name Paul had been last used in the seventeenth century by Paul V (1605–21), a member of the powerful Borghese family. But the new pope soon made clear that his choice was in honor of the great missionary and close associate of the apostles. Paul V had been a notable patron of the arts. His name was emblazoned on the facade of St. Peter's, which was completed during his pontificate. Many wondered what Montini's choice could mean.

The canopies were lowered as the pontiff was accompanied to the sacristy behind the sanctuary. Annibale Gammarelli, the papal tailor, had laid out white papal garments in three sizes. The master of ceremonies, Archbishop Enrico Dante, took charge of the protocol of dressing the new pope. Having changed into the white scimar, the caped ankle-length tunic, and the burgundy satin mozzetta, the new pontiff returned to take his place at the center of the sanctuary. The cardinals filed up to offer their required obeisance and loyalty.

The white smoke had billowed into the Roman sky. Gray at first, the smoke gradually paled into white clouds. The crowds in the square roared their approval even if they did not yet know the name of the new pope. With such a rapid conclusion it was assumed to have been either Lecaro or Montini. Cardinal Ottaviani made his way along the corridor leading from the Sistine Chapel to the central balcony of St. Peter's Basilica. As the red velvet drapes were pulled back, the elderly prelate stepped onto the loggia.

Annuntio vobis gaudium magnum: "I announce to you a great joy." *Habemus Papam*: "We have a pope."

The crowd, now close to 100,000, surged toward the facade of the basilica. The formula of words had been used since the election of Martin V in 1417 to communicate that an election was complete.

Emmentissimum ac Reverendissimum Dominum, Dominum Ioannem Baptistam, Sanctae Romanae Ecclesiae Cardinalem Montini, qui sibi nomen imposuit Paulum sextum. "The most reverend Lord, Lord John Baptist, of the Holy Roman Church, Cardinal Montini, who has taken the name Paul VI."

Within the hour the new pontiff appeared on the balcony and gave his first apostolic blessing, *Urbi et Orbi*, to the city and to the world. Paul had a clear idea of what the papacy required, having served three popes so closely. Protocol took over with the arrangements for the coronation, which was set for the evening of June 30.

The first days were a flurry of activity. The new pope took possession of the papal apartments, and congratulations poured in from all quarters. Preparations for the imminent coronation took up most of his time. The homily he would preach would be his first exposure to the wider Catholic world and would give an indication of the outlines of his pontificate.

A quarter of a million people packed into St. Peter's Square to witness the outdoor celebration that took place on the steps of the ancient basilica. The ceremony, broadcast throughout the world, began at 6:00 p.m. to avoid the torrid heat. The coronation, the last in papal history, was broadcast throughout the world on radio and newsreels. The two-and-a-half-hour ceremony combined the pageantry of the papal court with the ancient liturgical rites. The pope was crowned with a triple tiara, symbol of the palace, a gift from the people of Milan.

Already the previous day Pope Paul had announced that the council would continue. The work pace at the Vatican generally decreases during the oppressively hot months of July and August as most Romans take their summer vacation. But the early days of the Montini papacy were full of activity. Immediately following the coronation the pope received a number of heads of state and delegates. On Tuesday, July 2, the pope received in private audience President John F. Kennedy of the United States. During the formal speech the pontiff recalled meeting the young man almost twenty-five years earlier when members of the Kennedy family had attended the coronation of Pope Pius XII. On Wednesday, July 13, the pope held his first public general audience. A week later he traveled to the Quirinal Palace, once a papal residence and now the official seat of the Italian president, to exchange a courtesy visit.

The new pope soon settled into a routine. Each morning he rose at 5:30. After ablutions he spent an hour in prayer before Mass at 7:00 a.m. in his private chapel in the Apostolic Palace. Following a light breakfast, he went to his study shortly after 8:00 a.m. Documents from the Secretariat of State were delivered to his desk in a sealed pouch. The pontiff spent two to three hours reviewing the most important before beginning audiences at 11:00. These lasted until lunchtime, usually taken at 1:30 and always alone.

For the most part, the pope received bishops, nuncios, and cardinals. Bishops from various nations were obliged to make a visit to Rome every five years. Paul took a particular interest in their visits, meeting bishops individually and as a group. They provided him with an overview of the Catholic world.

After a brief rest and short walk in the Vatican Gardens, the pope received more visitors between 5:00 and 7:00 p.m.

Following evening prayers and supper, the pope retired to his study to read further documentation. He rarely retired before midnight, having spent three hours examining documents sent from the Secretariat of State.

Tuesday was officially set aside for his own recreation. Invariably Paul remained at his desk in the papal apartments, reading and composing speeches. Sunday afternoons were also reserved for his own personal reading and recreation. He enjoyed reading books on art in particular, a passion developed during his days as chaplain to FUCI. Paul had a deep interest in art and collected works that, although with little intrinsic value, were a gateway into contemplation of his Christian faith. In summer, and for a few days following Christmas and Easter, Paul spent his vacations at Castel Gandolfo.

On August 5 Pope Paul set out for the country residence, where he remained until September 12. The first seven days were secluded as he made a spiritual retreat. The task of reassembling the council awaited him. Among his first acts was the appointment, on August 10, of Giovanni Colombo as his successor as archbishop of Milan. On Wednesday, August 21, Paul began a series of weekly general audiences that he continued to maintain, uninterrupted, for the rest of his pontificate.

As the weeks passed Paul became surer of himself and his rapport with pilgrims. A talented linguist, he gradually added short greetings in diverse languages. In particular, he requested that people with any disabilities be placed near the dais so that they could have a clear view and that, when possible, he could greet them personally.

Throughout the summer Paul's overriding concern was the council and how to reconcile the various factions that had emerged. Having participated in the previous session,

Paul was acutely aware of the tensions between progressives and traditionalists. He had little idea how long the council would continue. Perhaps a further year could bring it to completion. During the summer months Paul worked to correct some of the organizational problems that had emerged in the first session. He invited lay members, all male, as well as representatives of other Christian churches, to participate as observers. In order to facilitate the work Paul suggested the reduction of discussion topics to seventeen.

Returning from Castel Gandolfo, Pope Paul presided over the opening of the second session of the council on September 29, 1963. The bishop-delegates of the world assembled at St. Peter's for the opening Mass presided over by Paul. During his homily, he expressed four hopes for the council: a discussion on the nature of the church, its renewal, its openness toward other Christians, and its openness to the contemporary world. In particular he expressed his desire that the council would not propose new dogmatic definitions but rather engage with the contemporary world.

During the council sessions, Paul formally took possession of the fourth-century cathedral of Rome, St. John Lateran. Paul was aware that he would be unlikely to attract the public affection that John had enjoyed. His reserved nature was in contrast to the expansive and extrovert John. Nonetheless, crowds flocked to see him. Paul did not attend the daily sessions of the council as his days were already full with audiences at the Apostolic Palace, receiving people who wished to meet the new pontiff. Each morning he received a myriad of small groups. The variety of such groups was extraordinary, and to each he gave a brief address. In the month of September alone he received university students, priests, politicians, visitors from Milan, the chancellor of Germany, and surgeons participating in an international congress, among countless other visitors. In addition, old friends from Milan and family members made occasional visits.

The issues discussed over the two-month session included the liturgy and communications. The renewal of the liturgy was the first issue to be addressed by the council fathers. The bishops were aware that the Latin liturgy, for all its sublime beauty, was largely lost on the lay faithful. They proposed a simplification of the liturgy and allowed for parts to be prayed and sung in the vernacular. The implementation was commended to the pope, and the changes in the liturgy were to have an unforeseen impact on the church for a further half century.

When Pope Paul closed the second session of the council on December 4, he promulgated the Constitution on the Sacred Liturgy and the Decree on the Mass Media. It was clear that at least another year would be needed to adequately discuss the issues on the agenda. Accordingly he told the bishops that they would assemble at the Vatican the following September.

As the bishops returned to their home dioceses, Paul turned to preparations for his first Christmas at the Vatican. Pope Paul visited the working-class parish of Pietralata, on the outskirts of Rome, where he celebrated Mass on Christmas Eve. The choice was deliberate. Since his days as chaplain to FUCI, Montini had a particular interest in the world of work and labor. Addressing the people, the pope explained that he wanted to come to an area that needed a paternal word of encouragement. Unemployment was high and crime was increasing. It was the first of many visits to the parishes of Rome. Throughout his pontificate he pressured civil authorities to provide adequate housing for the citizens of the city.

Although shy by nature and often overwhelmed by the crowds that surrounded his public appearances, Paul consistently tried to reach out to people. While lacking the spontaneity of Pope John, his sincerity was evident. In the first year of his pontificate, Paul tried to establish his own approach to the papacy and to guide the Second Vatican Council into its most delicate period.

CHAPTER FIVE

The Missionary Pope

Just before the second session of the Second Vatican Council ended in December 1963, Pope Paul VI made a surprise announcement in St. Peter's Basilica:

> I would now like to communicate something to you that we have had our hearts set on for some time . . . We are certain that in order for this Council to have a positive outcome, we must raise humble prayers and multiply our actions. After much reflection and having prayed a great deal to the Lord, we have decided to undertake a pilgrimage to that land which is the home of our Lord Jesus Christ . . . in order to recall the main mysteries of our salvation, that is, the Incarnation and redemption.[1]

Paul had been pope for just six months. But just three months after his election, Pope Paul had decided to explore the possibility of a visit to the Holy Land. In a handwritten note dated September 21, Paul expressed his hopes to make a short visit "in a spirit of piety, penitence, and generosity." His immediate task after election had been to continue the council that had been inaugurated less than a year earlier.

Preparation for the session consumed his time and energy, but he dispatched Monsignor Jacques Martin of the Secretariat of State and Monsignor Pasquale Macchi, his private secretary, to the Holy Land to explore such a possibility.

Despite innumerable problems, the plans for the first trip of the pontificate outside Italy went ahead. On January 4, 1964, Pope Paul left Rome bound for Amman, Jordan. After a formal welcome by King Hussein, the papal motorcade continued on to visit the place on the Jordan River where tradition maintains that Jesus was baptized by his cousin John.

From there the papal motorcade continued to Jerusalem, where Paul visited the Church of the Holy Sepulchre. The packed day concluded with audiences granted to several non-Catholic church representatives.

The following morning brought the pope to the Sea of Galilee and onward to Capernaum, where he visited the archeological site of the house where, according to tradition, the apostles Peter and Andrew lived. He then continued to the Mount of the Beatitudes before returning to Jerusalem.

The ecumenical high point of the trip was a formal meeting on January 6 with Patriarch Athenagoras of Constantinople. Rome and modern-day Istanbul had been separated for exactly 1,010 years. In 1054 the patriarch and pope had mutually excommunicated each other over issues more to do with prestige and politics than theology. Paul and Athenagoras embraced each other warmly. Commentators made much of the image of the successor of Peter meeting the patriarch so closely connected with St. Andrew. Thus it began a fruitful dialogue between Catholics and Orthodox, one that continues to this day.

Returning to Rome that evening, Pope Paul was greeted by enormous crowds in St. Peter's Square. The visit had been a huge success. To commemorate the journey and prolong its effect, some weeks later he decided to establish two institutes. The first was a school for children with impaired hearing and the second a center for ecumenical studies.

It was now time for Paul to turn his attention to the expansion of the College of Cardinals. With a consistory held on the feast of the Chair of Peter, the pope added twenty-seven new cardinals from various parts of the world. Shortly afterward Paul was visited with his annual bout of influenza, which required the canceling of several public events and a complete rest for ten days.

Lent began by celebrating Mass on Ash Wednesday in accordance with ancient tradition at the fifth-century church of Santa Sabina on the Aventine Hill. During his homily he praised the work of the council, in particular its recommendation to simplify the liturgy. He had yet to realize how dramatically the liturgy would be altered in coming years.

Paul invited the Redemptorist priest Fr. Bernard Häring to give a week-long Lenten retreat at the Vatican. Each Sunday of Lent the pope made a visit to a Roman parish, usually in the poorer areas of the city. His years of experience as archbishop of the largest diocese in Italy would stand him in good stead as bishop of the nation's capital city.

On March 12 the pope inaugurated a bronze statue of Pope Pius XII, designed by Francesco Messina, in St. Peter's Basilica. It was erected by the cardinals whom Pius had created, and Montini recalled that he had not been in that number. The statue stood directly opposite the monument commemorating Pope Pius XI.

On May 3 he celebrated Mass in the Chapel of Mary, Queen of Poland, beneath St. Peter's Basilica, and on May 15 he presided over a festive celebration of the millennium of Christianity. While he joined in the celebration he was aware that the church in Poland was severely tested and suffered severe persecution. Pope Paul's desire to visit Poland at the request of the Polish bishops remained unrealized. Despite his openness in dealings with the communist authorities, he knew that the Soviets would oppose a papal visit.

Some days later on May 7, 1964, Paul invited artists to meet with him in the Sistine Chapel. Although the church had been an important patron in the past, Paul was aware that painters, sculptors, musicians, and poets had been largely ignored. The assembled artists listened as the pope spoke with unexpected candor.

> We have caused you suffering because we imposed imitation as the primary canon on you who are creators, infinitely vivacious, spouting forth thousands of ideas and thousands of innovations. We—you were told—have this style and you must adapt to it; we have this tradition and you must maintain it; we have these teachers, and you must follow them; we have these canons, and there is no avoiding them. We can say that sometimes we have placed against you a leaden burden, please forgive us! . . .
>
>   We resorted to surrogates, to "oleography," to works of art of little value and less expenditure, also because, in our defense, we lacked the means to commission things which were great, beautiful, new and worth being admired . . .
>
>   Shall we make peace? Today? Here? Shall we be friends again? Might the Pope once again become a friend of artists?[2]

The latter months of John's reign had caused a cessation of much administrative work with which Paul needed to deal. One of his first administrative changes concerned an outreach to people of various religions. On May 17 Paul announced the establishment of a new Secretariat for Non-Christians, similar to the Secretariat for Christian Unity.

In China a cultural revolution was brewing, one that would find fruition two years later with the publication of the "May 16 Notification" by Chairman Mao Zedong. The communist leader ordered a systematic and brutal internal cleansing of the party. Over the following ten years millions of Chinese would be slaughtered for defending the "Four Old Things": traditional culture, ideas, traditions, and habits. The attack on the four values lasted a decade, and Christians were caught up in the "ten-year catastrophe." Never before in the history of humanity had such a systematic and vicious persecution of religious people taken place.

China had cut relations with the Holy See in 1949, and eight years later the Chinese Patriotic Catholic Association was founded. Since it did not respect the authority of the pope and looked only to the government, the movement was condemned by Pope Pius XII in July 1958.

Pope Paul deplored the separation of Chinese Catholics from the church. Relations with underground Catholics who had remained faithful to the pope were hazardous, and throughout his pontificate Paul tried to encourage the faithful Catholics to win back those who had joined the government-sponsored movement. His efforts met with no appreciable success, and underground Catholics faced persecution and death for their loyalty to Rome.

Addressing hundreds of Milanese pilgrims who marked the first anniversary of Paul's election on June 21, the pope rhetorically asked, "What links me to Milan?" He confessed his sudden departure was a cause of pain, for he had developed a deep affection for the city so close to his birthplace. He assured his listeners that he would never forget them. But there was little time for nostalgia as Paul faced the second year of his pontificate.

As Rome's summer heat swelled the pope withdrew in late July to Castel Gandolfo, where he remained for the remainder of the summer. In the serenity of the villa overlooking the volcanic lake of Albano, he dedicated himself to studying various documents and prepared for the forthcoming session of the council.

The sixteenth-century villa, acquired by Pope Urban VIII, lies sixteen miles southeast of Rome in the Alban Hills. Built on the ruins of the summer palace of the first-century Roman emperor Domitian, the villa had extensive gardens. Here the pope could relax on the cool terraces, although he maintained the same punishing rhythm of paperwork and received some members of the Curia.

Paul continued to welcome pilgrims on Wednesdays and to the recital of the Angelus on Sundays. In addition he granted audiences to special groups, young pilgrims in particular. With the third session of the council due to begin in the fall, these months were important to gather the vast documentation and prepare for the session that he hoped would conclude the council before Christmas.

On August 6 Paul issued his first encyclical, *Ecclesiam Suam*, on the theme of the church. It was memorable for its openness to dialogue with the modern world, leaving moral issues to be dealt with in freedom by the council. He refrained from making judgments on the global political situation, which some observers had expected.

There were occasional outings to the surrounding countryside. On August 11 the pontiff traveled to the town of Orvieto for a brief visit to the Eucharistic Congress. The following week, on the feast of the Assumption on August 15, Pope Paul celebrated Mass in the local parish church of St. Thomas and later visited the summer residence of Propaganda Fidei, the training college for seminarians from mission territories. On September 12, 1964, the pope bid farewell to the citizens of Castel Gandolfo and returned to Rome, where two days later he inaugurated the third session of the ecumenical council.

By now strains were showing clearly. The largely conservative Curia had wanted to control the council from the beginning. Their failure to do so had allowed a progressive wing to develop. At the end of the second session Cardinal Suenens had asked provocatively, "Why are we discussing the church when half the members are not even represented here?"

Stung by the criticism, Pope Paul appointed fifteen female auditors from as many countries, who along with other observers had no voting rights. The number was later raised to twenty-three. The vast majority of bishops appeared to be blithely oblivious of the sexist bias. In succeeding decades women were to outstrip men in their theological preparation and qualifications, as well as their articulation of contemporary issues of Christian concern.

Three themes dominated the third session: the church in the modern world, ecumenism, and Catholics of the Eastern Rite. Despite the reservations of some bishops, the tone of the documents was enthusiastic and showed a marked openness to the world.

Meanwhile, Pope Paul visited Montecassino on October 24, 1964. The hill town of Montecassino traced its Christian foundation to the fifth century when St. Benedict of Nursia founded an abbey. Both Benedict and his sister, St. Scholastica, were buried in the hilltop monastery. Pope Paul had long admired the contribution of the Benedictine Order to the church. The abbey had been entirely destroyed during the Second World War, when it was bombed by Allied forces. Rebuilt at the expense of the Italian government, the pope saw the completion of the work. During an elaborate ceremony the pope consecrated the newly rebuilt abbey church and proclaimed St. Benedict the patron saint of Europe. The pope brought five torches made by a contemporary artist.

Four were placed at the German, Polish, Italian, and Allied cemeteries, while the fifth was laid before St. Benedict's tomb. Despite the heavy rain, the pope insisted on driving through the vast throngs in the lower village to greet the thousands who had turned out along the streets.

The pope's word to artists found a concrete form when on November 1 he inaugurated the modernized private chapel in his apartments and decorated it with contemporary religious art. It was the first of several renovations of the papal chapels, which had varying degrees of success.

The first full year of the pontificate saw Paul's popularity continuing to rise. As the memory of John XXIII faded, Paul established himself as a paternal figure with simply a different manner from the late pope. The parish visitations were particularly appreciated by the Italians.

On November 13, the feast of St. John Chrysostom, the pope concelebrated Mass in St. Peter's Basilica in the Byzantine rite with the patriarch of Antioch, Maximos IV. At the end of the liturgy, the secretary general announced that the pontiff intended to donate the triple tiara used at his coronation to be sold for the benefit of the poor. The pope descended from his throne, took the tiara in his hands, and placed it on the altar before returning to his place bareheaded. Loud applause accompanied the arresting gesture. Sometime afterward Cardinal Francis Spellman urged some benefactors to buy the tiara, which was later donated to the museum at the National Shrine in Washington, DC.

The third session of the council concluded on November 21 and Pope Paul approved and promulgated decrees on each of the three topics discussed.

The pope had little time to digest the events of the council, however, for on December 2 he departed for Bombay, India, to attend the 38th Eucharistic Congress. Tens of thousands had gathered in the city to celebrate the festival, which takes place in a different part of the world every three or four years. This was Paul's second international journey, although the first visit of any pope to Asia. While not a state visit, the pope was accorded full honors, being greeted at the airport of Santa Cruz by Vice President Zakir Husain and Prime Minister Lal Bahadur Shastri.

On the afternoon of December 3 Pope Paul celebrated Mass at the Oval Stadium during which he consecrated six new bishops. Pilgrims had traveled from distant parts of the country and Paul was astonished at the vibrancy of the Indian church. The visit, announced only six weeks earlier on October 18, was an outstanding success. The people of India were impressed with the pontiff's gentle nature and humility. They were touched when he knelt to give children Holy Communion. His genuine delight at meeting so many people was apparent, and, at his request, he made visits to hospitals and Catholic schools. As he was shown to the ill and infirm, he embraced and blessed them. The pope had never seen such vast crowds, and people saw a tender side to Montini that had hitherto been hidden.

As the pope left Bombay he donated the car that had been used during the papal trip to an Albanian religious sister, Mother Teresa. The proceeds of the sale of the car were later given to the poor whom she served. Little could Pope Paul have known that half a century later a successor would canonize the diminutive sister as St. Teresa of Calcutta.

Returning to Rome, the pontiff was welcomed by thousands who lined the streets as the motorcade entered the Vatican. The prestige of the papacy had been strengthened, and the pontiff's popularity was at its peak. For the remainder of his pontificate, Paul would fail to maintain that public admiration and affection.

The council continued to occupy much of his time. Although the day-to-day running of the council was in the hands of delegates, the implementation of decrees remained his responsibility. Each evening he received a summary of the day's proceedings, which he studied assiduously, rarely retiring before midnight.

Eleven schemata remained unfinished at the end of 1964. The challenge was now to bring them to a conclusion by the end of 1965. The Council of Trent had met in three sessions between 1545 and 1563, and the decrees were then implemented by Pope Pius V (1566–72). With modern means of communication the bishops required a fraction of the preparation time of previous councils, and the pope encouraged the fathers to hasten toward bringing the council to a successful conclusion.

Paul was acutely aware of the advantage of regular meetings of the bishops. The council, for all its tensions, had shown the value of episcopal collaboration. Pope John XXIII had considered the establishment of an assembly. During the first session in 1963 the Syrian patriarch Maximos IV had forcibly suggested the establishment of such a body. It would, he argued, counterbalance the almost exclusive Western image of the Latin church. The patriarch proposed a rotating body of bishops resident in Rome and available to the pope for advice. Maximos was an ardent supporter of the celebration of the liturgy in the vernacular, and Paul was impressed by his scholarship. The pope suggested to the moderators of the council that such a synodal body should be considered.

On February 22, 1965, the pope created 27 cardinals during a consistory at the Vatican, internationalizing the college and raising the number of cardinals from 76 to 103. Among these were three Eastern Rite patriarchs. He simplified the ceremonies, which took place over four days. Among the new cardinals was Montini's old friend Giulio Bevilacqua, who insisted that he continue to work in his parish in Brescia and who continued to wear his old black cassock. The increased number of cardinals strengthened the links between the papacy and the growing number of Catholics throughout the world. In 1965 Catholics numbered some half a billion, and they outnumbered all other Christian traditions combined.

Paul was anxious to implement the decrees of the council. On the First Sunday of Lent, March 7, 1965, Paul traveled to the Roman parish of All Saint's, where he celebrated Mass in the vernacular, in Italian. This was the first time in centuries that Mass was celebrated in a language that everyone present could readily understand. In advance of the Mass, Cardinal Lecaro had spoken on television of the changes.

Apart from the language, the Mass was celebrated facing the people rather than the traditional *ad orientem*, toward the East. While the change was broadly met with popular approval, there were many critics who greeted the scaled-down liturgy with alarm. Ten days later, speaking at a general audience on March 17, the pope urged critics not to reject the liturgical changes and admonished those who opposed the new dispensation. The Easter ceremonies were also simplified at the Vatican and throughout the dioceses of the world. In a further step toward pluralism, on April 7 the pope established the Secretariat for Non-Believers to promote dialogue between Catholics and people of various religions and of none.

A month later, on May 6, Cardinal Giulio Bevilacqua, his old friend and confidante of his youth, died in Brescia. For several years Bevilacqua had shared his home, and Paul was greatly saddened by the personal loss. He had been an invaluable source of sage advice.

While he had opted not to undertake journeys until the council had concluded, Paul traveled two hundred miles to the northern city of Pisa on June 10 for a day visit to celebrate Mass during the National Eucharistic Congress. A heavily communist area, the pope received a warm welcome from the civic authorities and a rapturous welcome from the thousands of citizens and pilgrims.

Throughout the summer the pope put the finishing touches on his second encyclical letter, *Mysterium Fidei*, on the Eucharist. Paul published the letter on September 3, just days before the last session of the council began. The encyclical was a traditional survey of the centrality of the Eucharist that the decree *Lumen Gentium* declared was "the source and summit of the Christian life" (LG 11). The pope expressed concern about the imperfect understanding of the Eucharist in the minds of many people, clergy and faithful alike. He countered some of the theological developments that troubled him. The letter was largely overlooked by the secular press, however, and it was overshadowed by the opening of the final session of the council less than two weeks later.

As the bishops reassembled in Rome, Paul announced his intention to proceed with the establishment of the synod of bishops. He had decided against the model of retaining a rotating body in Rome. Rather he would summon representatives of the global episcopal conferences every few years to a plenary session. In the interim a secretariat would continue to provide a bridge between pope and bishops.

The first item for discussion was a decree on religious freedom, a document that ultimately became the most divisive of the conciliar documents. This was followed by *Gaudium et Spes*, an optimistic overview of the church in the modern world, and *Ad Gentes*, on missionary activity.

To mark his birthday on September 26, Pope Paul traveled to an international gypsy encampment at Pomezia outside Rome. Heavy overnight rain had put the visit in doubt, but the pope insisted on visiting the hundreds of nomads who lived in tents and provisional accommodation. Although the afternoon visit was curtailed, the pontiff insisted on walking through the mud to greet the people personally.

While the council was in session, Paul departed Rome for a short visit to America. The goal of the trip was not primarily the United States but rather the United Nations, still a relatively modest organization, which was due to celebrate its twentieth anniversary. The pope and his entourage left Rome's airport at 4:00 a.m. on a direct flight to New York. Given the change of time zone, the pope spent the longest day of his life, some thirty-two hours, in America.

The United States did not yet have full diplomatic relations with the Holy See. To many Americans, a relationship would compromise the separation between state and religious bodies. Although President Lyndon B. Johnson could not participate in a state reception, he was anxious to welcome the pontiff. A satisfactory solution was found when the president met with the pope at the Waldorf Astoria hotel in Manhattan.

The pope was greeted by thousands and received a ticker-tape reception on Fifth Avenue. In the late evening Paul celebrated Mass at Yankee Stadium, and on his way to the airport, he stopped by the World Fair, where Michelangelo's *Pietà* had been brought from the Vatican to be exhibited there.

During his address to the United Nations Pope Paul praised the work of the organization, in particular the Charter for Human Rights, before making an impassioned plea: "Never again war, never again war! It is peace, peace, that has to guide the destiny of the nations of all mankind!"[3]

Arriving back in Rome, Pope Paul went directly to St. Peter's to pray at the tomb of the apostle. The fathers were still in session at 12:45 when the pontiff arrived. "Never before has the evangelical mission had such a large audience, or been more willing to listen . . . to the message of peace," the pope enthused to sustained applause.[4] The welcome and courtesy extended outstripped Paul's expectations.

Five days after his return to the Vatican, the pope made the controversial decision to forbid the bishops from discussing obligatory clerical celibacy. He had already withdrawn the issue of artificial contraception and given it instead to a pontifical commission for study. These were issues that Pope Paul was anxious to defend from change.

Before the participants of the council left Rome, they gathered with the pope at St. Paul Outside-the-Walls, on December 4. It was the first time a pontiff took part in an ecumenical service. It showed what progress had been made in three years. The council concluded on December 8. There was an enormous feeling of euphoria as the pope bade farewell to the bishops and theologians. To each he confided a written message to be delivered to governments and people outside the Catholic Church. As the bishops returned to their dioceses, and the curial prelates to their offices, the task of correlating and implementing the decisions fell to the pontiff.

While the pope had put an optimistic gloss on the closing session, he could not disguise the fact that it had caused great division within the church. Nor could he foresee that the deepening antagonisms would lead to a schism in little over a decade. The most poignant moment had been when Cardinal Alfredo Ottaviani had made an impassioned plea not to change too dramatically the eucharistic liturgy. Partially blind, Ottaviani spoke from memory rather than read a prepared text. When he exceeded his allotted time, one of the cardinal presidents turned off his microphone to the delight of many bishops.

Paul entrusted the regional bishops with greater autonomy. By approving the role of the episcopal conferences, he tacitly consented to their limited independence. On November 23 that year, days before the council ended, Paul received the thirteen president-delegates of CELAM, the episcopal conferences of Latin America. Aware of regional tensions among the bishops, he indicated that their unified action would be more useful than factional divisions. He also agreed to travel to Latin America as soon as was practical.

Before the Polish bishops left Rome, they were received in private audience. Cardinal Stefan Wyszyński reminded the pope that the following year Poland would celebrate a millennium of the Christian faith. The bishops asked the pope to visit Poland if the political situation permitted. Recalling his brief sojourn in 1923, the pope agreed. Efforts to get the communist authorities to approve the visit failed, however, and the pope was obliged to celebrate the millennium in Rome.

Paul oversaw the various committees charged with implementing the changes introduced by the council. On February 17 Paul issued an apostolic constitution, *Paenitemini*, which modified the church's regulations on fasting and penance. A few days later on the feast of the Chair of St. Peter, Pope Paul held the first of the six consistories of his pontificate, in which he added twenty-seven new members to the Sacred College of Cardinals.

Giovanni Battista Montini had spent some three decades within the Roman Curia. He was aware of the defects of the system and the need for an improvement of standards. Last reformed in the late sixteenth century by Pope Sixtus V

(1585–90), the Curia needed to be modernized. Accordingly, Paul instituted a committee to overhaul the Roman Curia. On the ecumenical front Paul made progress. In March 1966, he received the archbishop of Canterbury, Michael Ramsey. His predecessor, Geoffrey Fisher, had met Pope John on December 2, 1960. But on that occasion not even an official photograph was issued. For John, ecumenism had been about inviting schismatics to return to the one, true church.

Paul received Ramsey in the Sistine Chapel, welcoming him "to your home, where you have the right to be." The shift in tone was noticeable. The next day the pair prayed at St. Paul Outside-the-Walls. Although the Catholic Church did not officially recognize Anglican orders, the pope gave the archbishop an episcopal ring while the pontiff received a pectoral cross. Both then signed a Common Declaration designed to reinforce the improved ecumenical atmosphere. The declaration was read aloud in Latin and in English. A joint theological commission was set up and an ecumenical center established in Rome whose task was to foster dialogue and explore united statements of agreed faith. The axiom of Pope John XXIII was invoked: "Seek what unites rather than what divides."

While the issue of artificial contraception had been assigned to a commission, the pope continued to implement the conciliar decrees. On June 14, 1966, Paul abolished the *Index of Forbidden Books*, an unwieldy compendium of prohibited authors and their works compiled to protect the faith and morals of the faithful. On August 6, 1966, in the *motu proprio Ecclesiae Sanctae*, Paul issued new regulations regarding bishops, priests, religious orders, vocations, and missionaries. The document was to have important repercussions as it began an era of change within the priesthood and religious orders. Many had been encouraged by the optimism stimulated by the council. That change was in the air was certain. How it was to be implemented was less sure. Within a few years the church was to experience an unprecedented exodus of clergy and religious from its ranks.

On September 1 Paul paid a surprise visit to the town of Fumone, seventy kilometers southeast of Rome, where he prayed at the tomb of Pope Celestine V, who had abdicated the papacy in 1294, after a pontificate of just four months. Observers wondered if the visit indicated the pope's intention to retire at a specified date in the future. It was only after Paul's death that it was revealed that he had prepared a letter of resignation in the event of incapacity to continue in the Petrine ministry.

Paul traveled to Florence by car to celebrate Christmas midnight Mass for the people of the city whose lives had been uprooted the previous month by devastating floods. It was the first time in living memory that such a ceremony was celebrated outside the Vatican. As he returned late that night on the three hour journey to the Vatican, the pope pledged financial support for a rest home to be built to house elderly couples.

According to tradition, St. Peter was martyred between the years 64 and 68. Pope Paul inaugurated a "Year of Faith" in 1967 to commemorate the martyrdom of the apostle under the rule of the emperor Nero. On February 22, the feast of the Chair of Peter, the pope published an apostolic exhortation, *Petrum et Paulum Apostolos*, a meditation on the lives and deaths of the two martyrs.

The priestly ministry was a constant care in Paul's thoughts. He was pained by the number of priests who applied for laicization. On February 24, with the *motu proprio Sacrum Diaconatus Ordinem*, he restored the permanent diaconate, which had fallen into disuse several centuries earlier. The diaconate was to take root in many countries and became an important anchor in parish life. Given his experience, Pope Paul intervened directly in the conflict that had led up to the Vietnam War, dispatching Paul Casimir Marcinkus to meet President Johnson with a handwritten letter calling for a ceasefire from hostilities. The president was committed to the war, which sought to limit communist activities in the region; hostilities continued for a further decade.

Paul was convinced that opposition to atheistic regimes was no longer sustainable. He fostered a warming of relations, already initiated by Pope John XXIII's overtures to the Russian authorities, and during his pontificate doubled the number of countries accredited to the Holy See. Working within such a bureaucratic system meant that Paul had to content himself with secondhand information fed in a series of memos from nuncios around the world.

Global peace relies on the observance of human rights. Already the United Nations' *Declaration of Human Rights* of 1948 had expounded upon the requirements to establish and maintain peace. Paul chose the theme for his fifth encyclical, *Populorum Progressio*, on the development of people. It was published on March 26, 1967. Earlier treatment of social problems by Paul's predecessors had been composed from a European point of view. Paul's encyclical, however, drafted by a group of theologians and sociologists from around the world, was an attempt to see problems and opportunities for development from various perspectives. Equitable social development and access to education, Paul argued, were the prerequisites for peace.

With the aid of many social analysts, Paul examined nascent globalization, noting that the poor were to remain victims of shifting economic systems. The document observed the new balance from East-to-West conflict to the inequitable distribution from North to South. Development, the pope asserted, is the new name for peace. Such views led to *The Wall Street Journal* dismissing the encyclical as "souped-up Marxism."[5]

Within the Catholic Church the encyclical was more warmly accepted. Many dioceses set up "Peace and Justice" committees that measured the development of the social goals. A number of national bishops' conferences established charities that specifically supported the work of human and spiritual relief services across the globe. At the Vatican, Paul established the Pontifical Council for Justice and Peace on January 6 to pursue themes of development of harmony and prosperity among the nations. It would remain one of the principal achievements of his reign.

Two months later the pope received Khoren I, Catholicos of the Armenian Apostolic Church, at the Vatican. The visit of the patriarch of the oldest Christian country in the world led to the establishment of interchurch dialogue and helped end centuries of mutual mistrust caused by theological and political differences.

In the postconciliar period there was much discussion about the relaxation of the Latin law of celibacy for the priests. While clergy in the Eastern Catholic rites could marry, in the West the prohibition had been in place for a thousand years. Paul was personally opposed to the relaxation of the rules. He sought to put an end to the debate surrounding the issue of celibacy with his encyclical *Sacerdotalis Caelibatus*, published on June 24. The discipline of celibacy was maintained, and no exceptions were to be made. Laicizations given to clergy who wished to leave the priesthood were obtained with great difficulty. The reaction to Paul's document was largely hostile. There were protests from many quarters and the period marked the beginning of a stream of clergy who opted to leave the ministry to marry.

Pope Paul made two international journeys outside Italy in 1967. The first was a day trip to Fatima in Portugal, where he met Sr. Lucia, a Carmelite sister who, along with two young cousins, claimed to have experienced a series of visions of Mary the Mother of Jesus in 1917. The occasion was the fiftieth anniversary of the apparition of Mary at Fatima. More than one million pilgrims from Portugal and Spain crowded the esplanade as the pope arrived at the sanctuary. In his homily he expressed the hope that the church would serenely accept the direction of the council. Aware that the tensions had not dissipated, he urged pilgrims to pray for God's guidance, invoking Mary's maternal protection.

In his second consistory, in which he created twenty-seven cardinals on June 26, 1967, Paul honored Poland by elevating the archbishop of Krakow, Karol Wojtyla, to the Sacred College. Paul had appointed him archbishop three years earlier in 1964, and it was traditional that the metropolitan of Krakow would become a cardinal. Paul had followed Wojtyla's career carefully and, having been impressed by a book he had written on the subject of married love, had appointed him a member of the commission to study the issue of artificial contraception. Wojtyla was prohibited from attending the meetings in Rome by the Polish authorities, however, so he submitted his observations to the committee in writing.

The outbreak of the Six Day War in the first week of June put a proposed pastoral visit to the largely Muslim country of Turkey in jeopardy. Having taken advice from international military sources, the pontiff went ahead with the visit, which took place July 25–26. At his first stop, the Cathedral of the Holy Spirit, the pope urged the bishops, priests, religious, and laity to work for the reunification of Christianity "in this city enriched by a glorious Christian past."[6]

Directly following the prayer service, the pope accepted the hospitality of President Cevdet Sunay, who accompanied him on a private boat trip along the Bosphorus. After a visit to the Museum of the Hagia Sophia, a former sixth-century church built by the emperor Justinian, the pope visited the patriarch Athenagoras, whom he had met three years earlier in Jerusalem. Hand in hand the two proceeded to the Church of St. George, where they prayed together and declared their unswerving efforts to bring about full communion between the two churches.

Montini's predecessor John XXIII had spent ten years, between 1934 and 1944, as apostolic delegate in Turkey. Greeting the diplomatic corps, the pope recalled with affection the service of his old friend and repeated the willingness of the Holy See to work with the political services.

Notwithstanding the temperatures that soared into the high nineties on the second day of his visit, the papal entourage visited Ephesus, the site of the great ecumenical council held there in 431. Here, with a voice almost overcome with emotion, he recited the Creed in Latin and the hymn in honor of Mary, *Salve Regina.*

Shortly before his trip to Turkey, Pope Paul abolished the Oath against Modernism, which had been introduced by Pope Pius X (1903–14) in 1910. The oath, taken by clergy and lecturers in theology, was designed to protect the faith against trends that worried Pope Pius. Paul's decision showed his desire for openness and scholarly research. The days of Modernist hunts were over.

On August 15 the pope published his long-awaited apostolic constitution, *Regimini Ecclesiae,* reforming the Roman Curia. With an intimate knowledge of the intricacies of the labyrinthine offices, Paul was well placed to oversee the reform. While some old departments were suppressed, the overall number was increased. The most substantial change was the expansion of members to include bishops and members of religious orders, appointed as advisors for a five-year period. This expanded the geographical representation in the Curia and, in theory, curbed the tendency of many to remain in ecclesiastical bureaucracy for their entire lives.

As part of the reform the pope tackled the prickly issue of Vatican finances. When the thousand-year-old Papal States were seized by the newly formed Italian government in 1870, Pope Pius IX had refused to deal with those whom he saw as usurpers. Only in 1929 was an agreement reached whereby the Holy See received recompense for properties and monies appropriated by the Italian state. As part of the agreement, Vatican City State, an area of 108 acres around St. Peter's Square, surrounding buildings, and various extraterritorial holdings were given to the Holy See. Little could Paul have foreseen that, some years later, this was to lay the groundwork for one of the greatest scandals of the modern papacy, the laundering of money by the Mafia and other criminals.

The first assembly of bishops, the synod of bishops, took place in the Vatican on September 29 to October 29. The theme of the synod, the first international meeting in the Latin church, was the preservation and strengthening of the Catholic faith.

Shortly before the synod was due to open, Paul experienced acute pain in his groin. After tests were carried out in a room in the Apostolic Palace, the doctors advised a prostate operation. As the synod was imminent, the pope requested that the operation be delayed until November. Notwithstanding the discomfort and fever, Paul put his energy into the final preparations for the historic convocation of representatives of the world's bishops.

To Paul's delight, Patriarch Athenagoras came from Turkey to take part. Arriving at St. Peter's Basilica while the bells tolled a festive welcome, the patriarch made his entrance to warm applause. Paul and the two thousand assembled bishops welcomed him while the patriarch placed a votive oil lamp before the tomb of St. Peter. The pope provided hospitality for the patriarch's stay in the fifteenth-century St. John's Tower in the Vatican Gardens. Writing a note of thanks following his visit to Pope Paul's private secretary Pasquale Macchi, the patriarch confided: "You are near to the greatest personality, not only of our Christian church but of all humanity."[7]

CHAPTER SIX

Paul and the Postconciliar Church

The year 1968 marked a dramatic change in Paul's pontificate both internally at the Vatican and on the world stage. The pope worked steadily to implement the decrees of the council. Aware that much of the ceremonial that surrounded the papal court was outdated, Paul simplified the day-to-day running of the papal household. In March he issued a *motu proprio, Pontificalis Domus,* streamlining many of the anachronistic elements of daily life at the Vatican. Several ceremonial titles and roles were made obsolete. The old Roman aristocracy, which had sided with Pope Pius IX's objection to the creation of the Kingdom of Italy, was abolished and all who had received papal court titles prior to the Lateran Treaty of 1929 lost their titles. This caused consternation and resentment among a loyal group of papal supporters.

The pope appointed his friend, the French diplomat, Jacques Martin, as prefect of the papal household. A further simplification of protocol came in June with the issuing of a *motu proprio* limiting the use of ecclesiastical decorations. But while these modest internal reforms were taking place, dramatic revolutions were breaking out in North America and across Europe.

In January young people in Paris mounted demonstrations against the perceived conservatism that limited their sexual expression. In March students rioted at the University of Warsaw when the communist government sought to ban a play that contained "anti-Soviet sentiments."

On April 4, the civil rights leader Dr. Martin Luther King Jr. was assassinated because of his nonviolent efforts to end racial segregation. Directly following news of his death, riots broke out across the nation. Some 150,000 people attended the pastor's funeral in Memphis on April 9. The next day the House of Representatives passed legislation to ensure civil liberties, signed into law as the Civil Rights Act by President Lyndon B. Johnson within twenty-four hours.

A month later, in May, a student revolution spread through several French cities. Soon workers joined in the spirit of rebellion as laborers demanded better working rights and pay. These manifestations were often violent, regularly engaging the police armed with tear gas. They were short lived, and by the end of July they had largely died out.

Earlier in the year, protests in Czechoslovakia to obtain freedom of the press and travel led to the invasion of the country by the Soviet Union and other members of the Warsaw pact to halt reforms. It was against this background that Pope Paul's diplomatic policy developed. Convinced that the divisions of Europe, where the East was dominated by the Soviet Union, were destined to last, he deemed it preferable to seek accommodation and avoid confrontation.

While he remained firmly opposed to atheistic communism, he was pragmatic in his efforts to find a "breathing space." It was, he believed, the best way to preserve the church from extinction in certain Eastern bloc countries. He dealt with nations through his nuncios on a state-to-state basis rather than through the national hierarchies. The decision to pursue this *Ostpolitik* had as much to do with Paul's temperament as his hopes to save the church in the East.

Paul concluded the "Year of Faith" on June 30 with the publication of his *Credo*, a meditation on the fourth-century Nicene Creed. He saw the document as a contribution to ecumenism in the spirit of John XXIII, seeking the common grounds of faith.

In the midst of this uncertain period the pope published, on July 25, an encyclical on human life and marriage. Having withdrawn the issue of artificial contraception from the discussions of the council, there was great anticipation that he would modify the regulations of the church. Instead, Paul chose a cautious approach, rejecting arguments, even from his papal commission, to modify the traditionally accepted church teachings put forth most recently in Pius XI's 1930 encyclical, *Casti Conubi*. In the controversial encyclical *Humanae Vitae*, Paul argued that artificial contraception would lead to marital infidelity and the loss of dignity of women and respect for life in the womb.

The unexpected storm of opposition provoked by *Humanae Vitae* had Paul reeling. While the secular press was predictably hostile to the rejection of artificial contraception, Paul was astonished by the vocal opposition from Catholics across the globe, and he interpreted the opposition as a personal affront.

Cardinal Carlo Maria Martini, archbishop of Milan (1980–2002), reflected on Paul's encyclical in the book *Night-Time Conversations in Jerusalem: On the Risk of Faith* (2008): "I knew Paul VI well. With the encyclical, he wanted to express consideration for human life. He explained his intention to some of his friends by using a comparison: although one must not lie, sometimes it is not possible to do otherwise; it may be necessary to conceal the truth, or it may be unavoidable to tell a lie. It is up to the moralists to explain where sin begins, especially in the cases in which there is a higher duty than the transmission of life."

The 39th International Eucharistic Congress in the Colombian capital of Bogotá provided the pope with the opportunity to visit Latin America. The news from Czechoslovakia worried him greatly, and he gave serious consideration to postponing his trip to another occasion. Meeting with Czech pilgrims the day before his departure to Rome, he stressed that he shared their preoccupation. Students in Belgrade, the capital of Yugoslavia, had held demonstrations against the government in the first week of June. These were violently crushed. On the night of August 20 a half million soldiers from the Soviet Union and its allies entered Czechoslovakia in order to halt liberalizing reforms introduced by Alexander Dubček, first secretary of the National Communist Party. Paul learned of the invasion while on his way to the airport to begin his four-day visit to Colombia.

Paul was aware of the complexity of the visit to Latin America. Since the Second World War several countries had been caught up in the Cold War and several had experienced military coups. Despite immense natural resources, many countries remained poor and undeveloped. Centuries of exploitation by Spanish and Portuguese slave traders, foreign administrators, and corrupt officials had reduced much of the population to poverty.

Corresponding to the political agitation, some church leaders had also challenged the status quo, protesting against the exploitation of the people and examining the unjust structures that oppressed and disenfranchised them. Latino theologians wrote powerfully about the injustice of such social discrimination. For many of these theologians, familiar with the crushing poverty so many suffered, poverty was the most extreme form of injustice.

Landing at Bogotá airport in a Boeing 707 after a twelve-hour flight, the pope knelt on the tarmac to kiss the ground. Having been greeted by the president and civil authorities, the papal cavalcade made its way through the crowded streets to the cathedral. Hundreds of thousands of Colombians and pilgrims gave the pontiff a near hysterical welcome. The pope stood in his open-roofed car for the forty-minute journey. Police reported that 536 people collapsed due to the suffocating heat.

The pope traveled in convoy to the site of the Eucharistic Congress close to the airport. During Mass the pope ordained 41 deacons and 161 priests from all over Latin America. Over a quarter of a million people were packed onto the grounds. Paul had appointed Cardinal Lecaro of Bologna as the papal legate, who had spoken eloquently in favor of the poor during the council. Paul's choice of legate underlined his conviction that the church should be ever-more at the service of the poor, whose rights were unjustly trampled on by unscrupulous potentates.

The following day the pope was formally received by the president and then went by helicopter to San José de Mosquera, eighteen miles from the capital. It was an extraordinary venue for a papal Mass. Tens of thousands of poor people, peasants, and farmhands crowded around the impromptu altar that had been erected in a field. During Mass the pope addressed the congregation affectionately: "You are a sign, a likeness, a mystery of Christ's presence. The sacrament of the Eucharist offers us His hidden presence, living and real. You too are a sacrament, a holy image of the Lord's presence in the world."[1] For an hour he journeyed through the excited crowds in a Jeep, pausing to bless and caress those whom he could reach. To underscore that the visit was to all sectors of Colombian society, the next morning the pope celebrated Mass in a poor parish on the outskirts of Bogotá and afterward visited two families in their homes.

On Saturday, before his departure, Paul inaugurated the second council of the bishops of Latin America, who met in the Colombian city of Medellín. Their deliberations were set against a backdrop of clergy who engaged in politics and fought for the social inclusion of the frequently exploited population of South America. These "Priests for the Third World" engaged in developing a strand of thought called liberation theology. Born in a flurry of postconciliar enthusiasm, the movement was not uniformly welcomed throughout the church. Some denounced the priests as Marxists, claiming that they were more interested in helping the poor in a material way rather than offering the sacraments. A gulf was to develop between the two polar positions and to last several decades.

Opposition to *Humanae Vitae* did not abate, stoked partly by the expectation that the church would relax its opposition to artificial contraception. Various episcopal conferences issued clarifications or commentaries, several of which subtly distanced themselves from Paul's views. The bishops of Canada were particularly vocal. It was the first time in the church's history that laypeople and clergy dissented so publicly from papal teaching. Cardinal Leo Suenens was his most formidable opponent. Paul was stung by the criticism from a man whom he had so closely trusted. Not only did Suenens disagree with the views expressed in the encyclical but he also insinuated that Paul had acted in an anticollegial way. Having raised the profile of the national bishops' conferences, Suenens was dismayed by the way Paul had paid scant attention to them. The cardinal spoke openly in television interviews, criticizing the pope's position.

For Pope Paul, acceptance of the encyclical was a matter of obedience to the magisterium, the teaching authority of the church. He was taken aback by the outcry against the issue of contraception, in particular the criticism by bishops and theologians.

The reception of the encyclical was affected by unprecedented social upheavals. Opposition to the war in Vietnam continued to provoke protests and demonstrations, notably in the United States. In Europe, a series of student revolutions swept the continent. The postwar period in Europe had seen a surge in the birth rate. Many young people rejected the moral and political values of their parents. Such disregard for traditional teaching baffled many church leaders.

On December 24, 1968, Paul visited the southern Italian city of Taranto. Over a half million people crowded into the streets of the coastal town. Some thirty thousand held flaming torches aloft as the pontiff motored to a steel plant to celebrate Mass with some fifteen thousand workers. A large slab of steel served as the improvised altar.

Pope Paul was unwell with an annual bout of influenza in the early part of 1969. He had improved sufficiently to receive US President Richard Nixon during his visit to the Vatican on March 2. President Nixon was permitted the unusual privilege of addressing seminarians and young priests in the Sala Clementina at the Apostolic Palace that evening. Nixon noted that often young people protest against things but find they have little to stand for. He urged the young clerics to put their talents to good use, in particular for the youth.

The third consistory for the creation of new cardinals on April 28 packed the College with Montini appointees. Only four of the thirty-four new cardinals were curial appointments, while the remainder were diocesan pastors from all over the globe. The increased number of cardinals and the geographical spread also acknowledged the growth of the church in Africa, Asia, and South America, giving the College more international depth.

The long, drawn-out reform of the liturgy was completed in April 1969 with the definitive promulgation of the revised rites of the Mass and sacraments, which would be published that following year. Paul used the Wednesday general audiences to explain the changes that the council had introduced. But already opposition was mounting to the mode and pace of the changes that the liturgical committee had introduced. The traditional Mass with Gregorian chant and polyphony had been replaced in some parts of the world by jazz and contemporary music. Reports to Rome catalogued various liturgical abuses. The liturgy, long a symbol of unity, became the focus point of bitter division.

Giovanni Battista Montini had retained a particular interest in labor relations dating back to his days as chaplain to FUCI. On June 10 the pope made a one-day visit to Geneva to address delegates on the occasion of the fiftieth anniversary of the International Labor Organization while also visiting the headquarters of the World Council of Churches. In a clumsy move, the pontiff avoided entering the ecumenical chapel, an oversight that offended several of his hosts.

In his address he repeated the commitment of the Catholic Church to seek full communion of faith with fellow Christians but cautioned against changing any Catholic doctrine.

The sight of a pope in Geneva, a symbolic city of Protestantism, was broadly welcomed by both Catholics and large swaths of the Reformed tradition. The visit was short in duration and limited in scope, but it was the first time a pontiff had greeted such a large ecumenical gathering outside the Vatican.

World history was made on the night of July 20/21 with the Apollo moon landing. Late that night Paul visited the papal observatory, located on the grounds at Castel Gandolfo. Through the telescope he gazed at the moon and later watched the live transmission of the moon landing. He exclaimed in his message to the astronauts: "Honor, greetings, and blessings to you, conquerors of the moon, pale lamp of our nights and our dreams. Today we celebrate a sublime victory."[2] Throughout that year, in advance of the anticipated landing on the moon, Pope Paul addressed the developments of science and its connection with religion. He received American astronauts Neil Armstrong, Edwin Aldrin Jr., and Michael Collins, along with their wives, during a private audience in the library of the Apostolic Palace.

Pope Paul made his only visit to Africa in 1969, the first visit of a pontiff in history. He chose Uganda, a country with a population of some three million Catholics. Uganda had gained independence from the United Kingdom in 1962, and the papal visit brought the highest ranking dignitary to date since independence.

On the afternoon of July 31 the pope's plane, escorted by four fighter planes in a guard of honor, touched down from Rome at Entebbe airport. The doors of the East African Airways Super VC10 opened and the pope appeared. Dancers in grass skirts and musicians with drums and traditional instruments performed a noisy welcome ceremony. The excited crowd watched as the pontiff descended the stairs and kissed the tarmac, and they immediately burst into song and ritual dance. Four presidents of African countries flanked the Ugandan president, Milton Obote, at the airport. Paul looked on quizzically at the unfamiliar rites of welcome and looked uncomfortable as garlands of flowers were hung around his shoulders. Women who normally dressed semi-naked for such occasions were attired more soberly as the pope began his visit.

Uganda was the location for a commemoration of twenty-three martyrs whom Pope Paul had canonized in a ceremony at the Vatican on October 18, 1964. With invitations to visit so many African countries Uganda offered the best opportunity to honor a vibrant church. On June 3, 1886, thirty-two young men, Anglican and Catholic, were burned to death on the orders of King Mwanga II, ruler of Buganda (former Uganda). The charge was their refusal to renounce their Christian faith, although their refusal to engage in sexual activity with the king and his courtiers may also have been a factor in their slaughter. The shared veneration of the martyrs by Catholics and Anglicans pointed to an improving ecumenical climate.

Following his arrival at Entebbe airport, the pope proceeded to celebrate Mass with the bishops of Africa at St. Mary's Cathedral. During his homily he addressed the role of Christianity on the continent, encouraging the Africans to see their faith as their own, rather than as a colonial religion imposed in earlier centuries. The pope expressed his desire to foster their identity as Christian and African. He cited native African theologians such as Augustine and Cyprian. The pope urged the Africans to be missionaries to each other, no longer relying on imported clergy and religious, and he encouraged the formation of lay catechists and an active laity. He then touched on the issue of enculturation, inviting Africans, drawing on their early history of Christianity, to adapt to the local culture.

The papal endorsement spread to the language and rites of Africans, which would stand in marked contrast to those imposed by the European missionaries of recent centuries. Paul's encouragement would have far-reaching effects and lead within decades to a rapidly flourishing church throughout the continent.

Paul was still troubled by the manner in which so many bishops had publicly contested the papal teaching in *Humanae Vitae*. In an effort to prevent further equipped dissent, Paul convened an "extraordinary" meeting of the synod of bishops in October with the theme "Cooperation of the Holy See with Episcopal Conferences." The meeting considered the role of bishops in their diocese. Paul underlined that all bishops were obliged to maintain unity with the successor of Peter. It was an attempt to rein in some of the bishops who displayed too much independence. A valuable lesson had been learned on both sides.

By now most of the reforms introduced by the council had been implemented, even if not all were universally welcomed. On September 25 Cardinal Ottaviani of the Holy Office wrote to the pope criticizing the apostolic constitution *Missale Romanum*, published on April 3, on the reform of the Mass. In a lengthy and subtly argued document Ottaviani, aided by several theologians, pointed out several grave breaks with the tradition of centuries. The clear indication was that the pope was falling into error, one of Paul's greatest fears.

Speaking at the general audience on November 26, 1969, Pope Paul acknowledged that the changes had upset some of the lay faithful and clergy. The Roman Rite had not been reformed since the Council of Trent in the mid-sixteenth century. "Understanding of prayer is worth more than the silken garments in which it is royally dressed. Participation by the people is worth more—particularly participation by modern people, so fond of plain language which is easily understood and converted into everyday speech."[3] Despite the misgivings of so many, however, Paul determined to press ahead with the publication of the new Roman Missal and follow this with renewed rites to accompany the other sacraments.

Some days earlier Paul had issued a document that dramatically changed future papal conclaves. As part of the reform of the Curia Paul had introduced the concept of a retirement age for bishops and heads of departments. On November 21 Paul delivered a coup de grace that incensed a number of members of the College of Cardinals. To their dismay, Paul set the ceiling of electors at 120 and prevented cardinals over the age of eighty from voting in conclave. Moreover, at that age, all cardinals ceased to be members of the curial departments. The norms, which took effect on January 1, retained the exclusive right of the cardinals to vote for a successor of Peter. The pope retained the tradition whereby the Roman pontiffs normally remained in office until death.

Social changes were also underway. At the pope's direction, prayers were offered in each of Rome's 432 churches "to spare Italy from the calamity of divorce." The Holy See, although separate and distinct from Italian politics, nevertheless, called on politicians to protect the indissolubility of civil marriage. On November 28 the pro-divorce side of the Chamber of Deputies, the Italian parliament, voted for a bill introducing divorce, which was ratified a year later on December 1 by the Italian Senate. For Paul, this was an affront to the waning role of the church in Italian society. The papal response was administered by the French cardinal

Jean-Marie Villot, whom Paul had appointed as secretary of state the previous May.

In 1970, Paul embarked on the longest and most ambitious voyage of his pontificate, a papal journey to Asia and Australia. Addressing dignitaries at Leonardo Da Vinci airport in Rome on the morning of November 26, Paul explained the motivation of his journey "to be a messenger of Christ among the peoples and nations of various historical origin, of important ethnicities and cultures, of various customs and regions."[4]

The papal plane stopped briefly for refueling at Tehran in Iran and again at Dacca airport in Pakistan. Two weeks earlier eastern Pakistan had been hit by a cyclone, leaving hundreds of thousands dead and an innumerable number displaced. The pope assured them that he had directed Caritas International to assist with funds, and he exhorted all Catholic charities to join in the efforts to help victims.

The pope continued on to Manila, arriving later that day. When he disembarked, he was greeted by a number of dignitaries. While shaking hands with them, a man dressed as a cleric rushed on him and pushed Paul with two heavy blows to the chest. The pope fell backward into the arms of his astonished entourage and slipped to the ground. As the pope regained his balance the man, dressed as a priest, was wrested to the ground by Monsignor Macchi, the pontiff's secretary.

Within moments the security personnel had arrested the man. A long, serrated knife, with which the deranged man intended to kill the pope, was found on the ground. Police later identified the assailant not as a cleric but a deranged Bolivian painter, Benjamin Mendoza y Amor.

The pope regained his composure and was accompanied by car to the cathedral for a ceremony. Only when washing his hands before Mass did he notice blood on his sleeve, without realizing that he had been injured.

In the early afternoon the pontiff traveled to the nunciature. There his doctor, Mario Fontana, carried out an examination. It was found that the knife had narrowly missed the pope's neck, protected as it was by a stiff linen collar. The two blows to the chest had left extensive bruising. Having given an anti-tetanus injection, the doctor urged Paul to cancel the remainder of the day's appointments as in addition to delayed shock, the doctor warned, there would probably be fever. The pope refused to modify the program and received the diplomatic corps before traveling to the presidential palace for an official welcome later that afternoon.

In a written note, the pope later stated that he initially believed the accident was caused by an overzealous cleric. The intervention of a protocol aid, Monsignor Paul Casimir Marcinkus, a native of Chicago, was noted, and on future trips he acted as an unofficial bodyguard.

Given his geographical proximity to war-torn Vietnam, the next day the pope made an appeal for peace. He visited the Pontifical University of San Tomas, where he was welcomed by children from thirteen Catholic schools and a number of university students. He later broadcast a radio message in English to mark the first visit of a pope to the Far East. Noting that half of the world's population resided on the Asian continent, the pope called on the people to improve their social and economic situation through work and to offer care for the impoverished in the region. While he praised the advances brought by scientific discoveries and technological advances, he urged his listeners to avoid the lure of empty materialism.

The following day, November 28, Paul gave First Communion to a number of children at Luneta Park in Manila, and he presided over an ordination ceremony of 189 deacons before a crowd of some two million worshipers. Given his exalted view of the priesthood, Paul was deeply affected by the large number of priests who left the active ministry in the years directly following the council. Addressing the ordinands, he reminded them of their task: "All classes of people seem to stretch out their hands to [the priest] and to ask for his understanding, his compassion and his assistance: children, young people, the poor, the sick, those who hunger for bread and for justice, the unfortunate, the sinners—all have need of the help of the priest. Never say that your lives are irrelevant and useless."[5]

Speaking at Mass at Quezon Circle early the next day, attended by close to a million people, the pope posed the question of how the teaching of Christ may help contemporary humanity: "In its positive aspect it unleashes incomparable and unquenchable moral forces; in its negative aspect it denounces all forms of selfishness, inertia and forgetfulness which do harm to the needs of others. Christ proclaims the equality and brotherhood of all men: who but He has taught and can still effectively teach such principles which revolution, while benefitting from them, rejects?"[6]

The most touching moment of the two-day visit to Manila came when Pope Paul greeted a number of families in a slum area. The pontiff celebrated Mass at Tondo, one of the most impoverished areas of the city. Aware that few could get a glimpse of him, he asked to visit a number of poor people following the Mass. An open-air truck brought him through the district. Without warning, the pope asked the truck to halt so that he could disembark.

The elderly pontiff walked along the mud paths leading to the corrugated iron and wooden shacks. Entering a small hovel, the pope greeted a couple along with their ten children. Bystanders were astonished at the impromptu visit while the children played on the floor. The pope surveyed the scene quietly and blessed the occupants.

From Manila the pope continued to Samoa, an island halfway between Hawaii and New Zealand in the Polynesian region of the Pacific Ocean. While Catholics comprised less than one-fifth of the country's population, the majority of the islanders had converted to some form of Christianity. The ten-hour plane journey gave the pope a chance to rest while the day-long visit provided Paul with an opportunity to address the need for enculturation. Speaking in Samoa, he acknowledged the work of the foreign missionaries, praising their personal sacrifices to live out the Gospel message authentically.

The penultimate stop of the pastoral voyage was Australia. Given the vast scale of the continent, the pope remained in Sydney for three days, during which he celebrated Masses at St. Mary's Cathedral and Randwick Racecourse as well as a special Mass for Catholic schoolchildren and university students.

The second day of the visit opened with a visit to institutional homes for sick children and for the elderly. Mass at Randwick, attended by a quarter of a million people, commemorated the bicentenary of the landing on Australian soil by the English mariner Captain James Cook, who claimed the east coast for the British crown in 1770. Following the Mass, the pope met with ecumenical leaders of various churches at Tower Hall. It was still unheard of for Christian leaders to attend a Catholic Mass. The media coverage of the first visit of a pope to Australia was positive. On the final day Pope Paul conferred episcopal ordination on Louis Vangeke, the first bishop of New Guinea.

From Australia the pope continued to Djakarta, Indonesia. After another ten-hour flight and finally succumbing to a fever brought on by the anti-tetanus injection, Paul collapsed following a visit to the local cathedral. Once more he defied his personal physician and continued on to meet the president before celebrating Mass at the stadium with a crowd of 100,000 worshipers, who lit small votive lamps that illuminated the night air.

The following day the papal entourage left for Hong Kong on the final leg of the journey. Politically, the visit was a delicate one. For close to two decades the communist authorities had forbidden Catholics to worship openly in China. Paul celebrated Mass in public and extended an affectionate greeting to the people of Hong Kong and nearby mainland China. Unable to visit the country itself, he expressed the hope that someday he would return.

But this was to be the last long journey of his pontificate. After a seven-hour flight to Colombo, Sri Lanka, where he celebrated Mass at the airport, the pope returned to Rome. Although physically exhausted, Paul appeared at the window of his study at the Apostolic Palace the day following his return to recite the Sunday Angelus. He could not hide his disappointment at the legislation introduced to legalize divorce, which he named as "an unhappy development for the Italian family."

One of the most important, if unforeseen, fruits of the Second Vatican Council was the flourishing of a number of ecclesial movements of the lay faithful. One of the key phrases in the council documents was that of the "People of God." The church was seen as a river of humanity nourished by countless streams. The people of God, listening to the message of the Gospel and reading the signs of the times, continued to establish the kingdom of God brought by Jesus. While many of the great traditional religious orders and congregations had lay associates, or tertiaries, a number of new movements were founded for and governed by laypeople.

Opus Dei had been founded by the Spanish priest and later saint Josemaria Escriva de Balaguer in 1928, and members resonated in particular with the call of the council for Christians to influence society at all levels. The Legion of Mary had been founded in Dublin by Frank Duff in 1921, but in the years following the council had expanded globally. The Focolare movement gathered around the person of Chiara Lubich in the Italian town of Trent. Lubich had founded the group in 1943. Apart from their dedication to unity in Jesus, they also played an important ecumenical role across the Christian churches.

Milan was the home of Communion and Liberation, founded by the Italian priest Don Luigi Giussani. This ecclesial movement developed from the student movement. Within the group were members of the *Memores Domini*, people who took vows of poverty, chastity, and obedience. Following the introduction of divorce in Italy, the political profile of the movement developed dramatically.

The Neocatechumenate movement, founded by Francisco Argüello and Carmen Hernández in Madrid, was a parish-based movement that laid special emphasis on the call of baptism for every Christian. Members seek to revitalize parishes that have grown jaded.

The Charismatic Renewal Group had its roots in the spiritual experiences of the early Christians but had greatly expanded throughout the Christian churches in the twentieth century. This group contributed to the development of ecumenism and made a dramatic impact on those who embraced the energy that the movement provided.

The growth of all these groups for Paul was proof of the spiritual fruits of the council and provided a welcome antidote for the waves of secularism in the contemporary world. Paul became convinced that this mundane spirit was adversely affecting Catholics. In his homilies and addresses he increasingly admonished Catholics to avoid worldly temptations.

Paul's visit to the Far East was the last overseas journey of his pontificate and the final visit outside the borders of Italy. While he continued to make shorter journeys within his native country, the logistics of providing security and his advancing age, now aggravated by arthritis, led Paul to decline invitations for further pastoral visits abroad. The international visits had served not only to raise the profile of the papacy in the host nations but through television and the printed media made the white-robed figure ever more a familiar global figure. But it was now time to remain at home and welcome the increasing influx of pilgrims from every part of the globe.

In 1966 the Italian architect Pier Luigi Nervi had begun the construction of a new audience hall, with capacity to seat eight thousand visitors, on the site of a nineteenth-century hospital on the periphery of Vatican City, close to the perimeter walls. It was completed five years later and inaugurated on June 30, 1971. The ultramodern hall could comfortably cater to visitors with special needs. A space was included to house the synod of bishops during their tri-annual meetings.

The year (1971) marked a personal tragedy with the sudden death of Paul's brother Francesco from a heart attack. Unable to attend the funeral in Milan, Paul invited the family to the Vatican, where a month later he celebrated a Requiem Mass in the private apartments.

Paul aided the Hungarian cardinal József Mindszenty, who had lived at the American embassy in Budapest since 1956. He had claimed political asylum, having suffered physical torture at the hands of the communist Hungarian government. The internment followed the invasion of Soviet troops on November 4 of that year. By the late 1960s Mind-szenty's health had seriously deteriorated. The political situation had changed over the period and the communist authorities now feared that Mindszenty's death could create an unwelcome martyr. Pope Paul recommended that Mindszenty should leave the American compound. Reluctantly the Hungarian primate accepted Paul's invitation to travel to Rome, where Paul greeted him at St. John's Tower in the Vatican Gardens and housed him there. With difficulty, Paul persuaded Mindszenty to remain in Rome.

The eightieth anniversary of Leo XIII's encyclical *Rerum Novarum* on social themes provided Paul with the opportunity to contribute his own thoughts in the apostolic letter *Octogesima Adveniens*. Surveying the immense work of charities, Paul urged every Christian to actively contribute to social justice by engaging in practical efforts to support the poor. Such assistance was not simply to consist of charitable donations but to address the systemic roots of social inequality. Paul also urged humanity to preserve the environment from industrial pollution and hand it on intact to future generations.

The second ordinary session of the synod of bishops met at the Vatican September 30 to November 6, taking the ministerial priesthood and global justice as its twin themes. At the opening Mass where Mindszenty was the principal concelebrant, Paul praised the primate for his heroic stoicism in the face of state persecution.

The theme of social justice took up concepts dealt with by Paul in *Octogesima Adveniens*. As the concept of the synod was relatively new, no decision had been made as to how to record and publish the minutes. The delegates were split between publishing their own views of the proceedings and inviting the pope to compose an apostolic letter. In the event neither was followed but the delegates decided to confine future synods to simply one theme.

On October 17, in a ceremony imbued with political overtones, the Polish Franciscan friar Fr. Maximilian Kolbe was beatified by Pope Paul in St. Peter's Square. The priest had perished at Auschwitz in 1941. Following the escape of a prisoner, ten inmates were taken by the German commander who ordered that they be starved to death. The punishment was designed to deter others from attempting to flee. Kolbe, however, volunteered to take the place of one of the ten who protested that he had a wife and children. Over the two weeks the ten died. Kolbe was the last to perish, receiving a lethal injection of carbolic acid. His body, along with those of the other victims of the camp, was cremated.

In 1972, speaking to a delegation of the Year of the Book, initiated by UNESCO, Pope Paul expressed his admiration for the world of literature. His speech reflected the importance literature and writing played in the life of Giovanni Battista Montini, who as priest, bishop, and pope had labored both in composition and in reading texts that expressed the church's mission. Although assisted by the Curia, the pope was obliged to process an enormous body of writing. It was a challenge to which he responded with increasing difficulty.

Now in his mid-seventies, the pope was no longer able to adjust rapidly and provide responses demanded by the administration, although he insisted that everything pass across his desk. When the synod council met in early spring, the deliberations were sent to the pope for approval. Paul vacillated between five subjects—marriage, evangelization, the teaching office of the church, the diocese, and the pastoral care of youth—before finally deciding in favor of evangelization.

On June 29, Paul marked the ninth anniversary of his pontificate. Given his failing health, the pope had composed a letter of resignation to be implemented if he suffered an irreversible health crisis. He was afflicted by arthritis and his mood was often despondent as he received reports from around the globe sent by people who disagreed vehemently with the path of the postconciliar church. That evening, Paul celebrated the feast day of St. Peter and St. Paul and preached a morose sermon. He gave a pessimistic view of the state of the church. In an oft-quoted line, he rhetorically asked if through some fissure the smoke of Satan had entered the temple of God. Rather than bask in the glory of the recent council, Paul noted that a state of uncertainty seemed to pervade the church: "While there was a belief that after the Council there would be a day of sunshine, instead the clouds arrived, bringing tempests, darkness and doubt."[7] This was to be a leitmotif of the remaining years of his papacy.

Earlier in the year, speaking with the parish priests of Rome on February 17, Paul had mulled over the dramatic changes that had taken place in the priesthood in just a few years. The rapidly declining numbers in some places, the abandonment of religious dress, and the challenging of ecclesiastical authority deeply disturbed him.

On Sunday, September 16, Paul visited the city of Udine in the north of Italy at the close of the national Eucharistic Congress. In the late afternoon he traveled to Venice. Meeting the patriarch, Cardinal Albino Luciani, the pontiff took the stole from his own shoulders and placed it on the neck of the patriarch. Six years later Luciani was elected Paul's successor.

As the year drew to a close, on December 24, the pope visited the small village of Ponzano Romano in the province of Lazio outside Rome. Foregoing the splendors of St. Peter's

Basilica, the pope chose to celebrate Christmas Midnight Mass with the local inhabitants in a simple suburb of the city. Paul had accepted the invitation of the local priest to celebrate the Christmas liturgy. As the pope left the parish church, he invited the choir to come sing at the Vatican.

The longed-for end to the hostilities in Vietnam was announced on January 23, 1973. The pope learned of it the next morning and issued a message celebrating the establishment of peace between the United States of America and Vietnam, as well as offering consolation to all who had suffered during the war. Funds were transferred to Vietnam to assist in the restructuring of the national infrastructure.

A long-cherished dream came to fulfillment during the summer of 1973 when on June 23 Pope Paul inaugurated the Gallery of Contemporary Art within the Vatican Museums. All his life Montini had a deep interest in art and aesthetics and had collected a number of artworks. Although neither of great financial value nor artistic merit, these formed the nucleus of the gallery. Paul charged his secretary Pasquale Macchi to carry the project forward. Macchi contacted many artists and the families of deceased artists requesting donations. While the policy succeeded in acquiring paintings and sculptures, the quality of the pieces generally had little commercial value.

In line with the ecumenical overtures made by the bishops at the Second Vatican Council, Paul continued to develop links with other Christian churches. In this he was aware of the importance of example. The visit of Pope Amba Shenouda III of the Coptic Church in May of that year allowed both churches to sign a common declaration. It was a further step on the road toward unity.

Montini had the satisfaction of a small diplomatic triumph when in July the Holy See was invited to take part in an international governmental conference on European security. The church had been effectively excluded from European politics at such a level since the Congress of Vienna in 1815, and this was an opening for the Holy See to take its place, at least as an observer, in several international institutions.

As he passed the tenth anniversary of his election to the pontificate, Paul's status in Italy slipped in the media and in political circles. With just a year to run before the opening of the holy year of reconciliation and a synod to open in the fall of 1974, Paul's calendar was full. And yet the usual chores of a papal year remained to be carried out as normal. The onerous task of organizing the synod was assigned to a council but Paul continued to micromanage the preparations. Throughout the summer he oversaw the formation of the committees and delegates that did not meet until Paul inaugurated the session in September.

The synod's theme, spreading the Gospel in contemporary society, seemed innocuous but was to have profound implications. In the years immediately following the Second Vatican Council there had been a lull in missionary activity. A popular interpretation indicated that all were saved by Christ, "anonymous Christians" (in the phrase of the German Jesuit Karl Rahner), who did not require evangelization. Paul chose Cardinal Karol Wojtyla as one of the five general relators. The position gave Wojtyla unprecedented exposure as he came to the attention of the international delegates; it was Wojtyla who set the agenda and oversaw the summation. The synod was the beginning of Wojtyla's path to the papacy.

Five years earlier, while Paul was in Oceania on a pastoral visit, the Italian parliament had ratified a law that permitted divorce. A number of lay Catholics, including Gabrio Lombardi, Sergio Cotta, Augusto Del Noce, and Giorgio La

Pira, challenged the law and proposed a referendum. The plebiscite was delayed until May 12, 1974, when the proposal to eliminate divorce was rejected by some 60 percent of the population. For several years Italian politicians had debated the merits of introducing divorce into civil society. The Catholic bishops and clergy vehemently defended the institution of marriage in both its spiritual and civil forms. The Italian church stepped up its opposition to divorce as it readied for legislation due to be introduced by the government in the spring.

Paul was dismayed at both the decision of the people to allow divorce and the implied detachment from church teaching. Celebrating Mass on June 8 of that year with the Italian bishops, Paul expressed his disappointment:

> We will make a paternal appeal to the ecclesiastics and religious, to the men of culture and action, and to the many dear faithful and secular of Catholic upbringing who have not taken into account, on this occasion, the fidelity due to an explicit evangelical commandment, to a clear principle of natural law, to a respectful reminder of ecclesial discipline and communion, so wisely enunciated by this episcopal conference and validated by ourselves: we will exhort all of them to bear witness to their declared love for the Church and to their return to full ecclesial communion, exerting themselves with all their brothers in faith in the true service of man and his institutions, so that these may be internally ever more animated by the authentic Christian spirit.[8]

The changes spreading throughout Western society seemed unstoppable while reports from various parts of Europe confirmed that regular church attendance was diminishing at an alarming rate. Paul became concerned about the breakdown in morality that he perceived around the globe, and was distressed by the recent views on abortion and marriage in Italy. Meeting with the International Theological Committee for a plenary session at the Vatican in December 1974, the pope asked the members to work on the theme "Sources of Christian Moral Conscience." In his speech he pessimistically surveyed the world where traditional Christian values were retreating.

Meanwhile Paul was faced with growing financial problems within the Holy See. The expanded Curia required an increasing amount of money. The Holy See had an income from the settlement in the 1929 Lateran Pact and a tax from various dioceses and religious congregations. Paul had decided to divest some of the funds that had been invested solely in Italian interests and spread them globally. One of his chief advisors was Archbishop Paul Casimir Marcinkus, who had been appointed secretary to the Institute for the Works of Religion, commonly but incorrectly called the Vatican Bank. Paul's admiration for the bluntly spoken American reflected his desire to broaden the reach of finances beyond the shores of Italy but also led the Holy See into both financial difficulty and a series of scandals that would reverberate for a further half century.

Paul's other chief advisor was a Milanese financier, Michele Sindona. Both were to later prove disastrous for the finances and reputation of the Holy See, inflicting almost irreparable damage. Marcinkus survived into the pontificate of John Paul II, although he was forced to resign his position. Sindona was poisoned in 1986 while serving a twenty-five-year prison sentence for the murder of Giorgio Ambrosoli.

The holy year of 1975 had occupied Paul's thoughts for much of the previous year. The first jubilee year had been celebrated in 1300 under Pope Boniface VIII (1294–1303), and fifty years later Pope Clement VI (1342–52) decreed that the jubilee should be celebrated at an interval of fifty years. In 1425 Pope Martin V (1417–31) reduced the period to twenty-five years. The last jubilee, or holy year, had been celebrated under Pope Pius XII in 1950. That occasion had been a huge success, as large numbers of people across war-torn Europe participated in colossal events overseen by a pontiff who clearly enjoyed the adulation of the crowds.

A committee had been formed to prepare for the millions of pilgrims expected to flock to Rome in 1975. Already, when Paul announced the convocation of the holy year at a general audience on May 9, 1973, he preempted those who wondered if such an event was anachronistic. The theme would be reconciliation with God and with each other.

Archbishop Annibale Bugnini, the architect of the liturgical reform movement, left his post as secretary to the Congregation for Divine Worship in July 1975. Months later he was appointed as apostolic delegate in Iran, a posting for which he had few qualifications. It was a classic maneuver of promoting a cleric in order to remove him. The abrupt departure may have been either complaints against Bugnini's reform or rumors that he was a member of the proscripted Freemasons.

In the late evening of Christmas Eve 1975, hundreds gathered in the atrium to witness the opening of the holy door, bricked up by Pope Pius half a century earlier. Paul processed to the door to the right of the atrium. Striking the silver plaque at the center of the portal, he intoned the words of the psalm, *Aperite mihi portas justitiae*, Open to me doors of justice. As the enormous slab behind the door was lowered from inside the basilica, the pope narrowly missed injury from masonry falling from the upper doorjamb. Shaken, the pope waited while the door was pulled open from inside. Millions of viewers watched the spectacle, choreographed by the director Franco Zefferelli.

Part of Paul's vision was to display the wonders of Rome for the vast amount of pilgrims expected to swarm the streets of Rome in the millions. It was also the tenth anniversary of the close of the Second Vatican Council. At the distance of a decade it was time for some to review the manner in which the decrees of the council had been executed. Not all judgments would be favorable. In the intervening years, most of the conciliar decrees had been largely accepted. Some, such as a renewed emphasis on ecumenism and relations with other religions, failed to stir up much enthusiasm. While rituals and liturgies were adapted into vernacular languages, tensions arose between those who wished to retain the status quo and those who wished to develop and explore new ways of worship.

Huge crowds flocked to Rome, with estimates between seven and eight million pilgrims. Improved methods of transport and expanding globalization allowed vast multitudes to come to Rome. The Easter ceremonies were attended by hundreds of thousands of pilgrims, and, thanks to the advent of television, many of the ceremonies were broadcast live throughout the world. In addition to the regular ceremonies, visitors and viewers were able to participate in the canonization of Elizabeth Ann Seton, the first American-born saint and convert, and St. Oliver Plunkett, the Irish archbishop of Armagh slaughtered for his faith in the seventeenth century.

The jubilee year fell during the United Nations International Women's Year and against the backdrop of a debate within the Anglican Communion regarding the admission of women to ministry. The call for the ordination of women in the Reformed churches was echoed by many within the

Catholic Church. The archbishop of Canterbury, Dr. Donald Coggan, corresponded with the pope over the issue. Two years earlier eleven women had been ordained in a controversial service in Philadelphia by three Anglican prelates and four more in Washington in 1975. Although judged illicit, the ordinations gave impetus to the General Synod of the Anglican Communion of Canada to approve female ordination to priesthood.

In December Paul published the apostolic letter *Evangelii Nuntiandi*, summing up the conclusions of the recent synod. The document made an immediate distinction from past practice where priests and religious were the principal missionaries. Now the task of spreading the Gospel was to be shared by all the baptized. The document, of which one of the ghost writers was Cardinal Wojtyla, dealt with the way in which the Christian faith is to be shared and also considered the place of Catholicism alongside other denominations and religions. The document was widely welcomed by the public as well as many academics as it marked a shift in emphasis from clerical missionaries to the priesthood of all the baptized.

Throughout the year the pope welcomed large crowds to special ceremonies and the general audiences to which he dedicated a special catechesis. Those who had traveled farthest to reach Rome were seated closest to the pope. When the year concluded at Christmas, the pontiff was exhausted but enthused by the energy generated by the throngs who flooded the Eternal City.

CHAPTER SEVEN

A Pontificate Drawing to a Close

During the opening months of 1976 papal audiences were reduced to allow the elderly pontiff a period of rest. In March Cardinal Karol Wojtyla preached the annual retreat to the Roman Curia and the pope. Twice each day for a week the Polish prelate gave a meditation in the Matilde Chapel of the Apostolic Palace. As the Curia attended within the chapel, the pope listened from the adjacent sacristy. It was a mark of favor toward both Poland and its illustrious son.

Paul's general health continued to decline slowly. Approaching his eightieth year, he needed to conserve his energy to govern the vast expanse of the church and relied increasingly on his Curia. In particular he leaned on the *sostituto*, Archbishop Giovanni Benelli, who took care of the day-to-day running of the closing pontificate. In the papal apartments, he relied increasingly on the young Irish missionary priest Fr. John Magee, who had come to assist the elderly pontiff during the jubilee year. But Paul could not abrogate his responsibilities and one last challenge required his personal intervention. Despite his failing health, Paul felt obliged to intervene in a dispute concerning a small group of dissidents who threatened his authority. The challenge was led by a gently spoken but iron-willed French bishop.

Marcel Lefebvre was born in 1905 in Tourcoing in northern France. Having entered the diocesan priesthood, he became a member of the missionary congregation of the Holy Ghost Fathers and worked in Gabon. In 1947 he was consecrated bishop and appointed apostolic delegate for French-speaking West Africa. In 1962 he was elected superior general of the Holy Ghost Fathers and later participated in the Second Vatican Council.

Although a drafting member of the council's central committee, Lefebvre grew increasingly suspicious of trends that he perceived as out of step with tradition. He took a leading part in a group of bishops who tried to prevent many of the decisions of the conciliar fathers from being implemented. Lefebvre's intransigence gained him many enemies, not least among the Holy Ghost Fraternity, who isolated him to the extent that he resigned as superior general.

But the French ecclesiastic also gained significant followers. In 1970 he opened a seminary in the Swiss town of Ecône to train seminarians in accordance with tradition. Although he initially had the permission of the local bishop, Lefebvre was increasingly critical of the direction in which the church was moving. The abandonment of religious garb, modern music in the liturgy, and liturgical abuses convinced him that the church was becoming dangerously secular.

Already the previous year Paul had dispatched to Ecône three cardinals, Gabriel-Marie Garrone, Arturo Tabera, and John J. Wright, who recommended that the local bishop withdraw his support for the seminary. Paul wrote personally to Lefebvre, in French, on June 29 that year urging him to desist from his intention to carry out illicit priestly ordinations.

The Congregation for the Bishops imposed restrictions on Lefebvre's work at Ecône. Portrayed at the Vatican as a rogue bishop, he was seen by many as a brave champion of orthodoxy. After a visitation of the seminary by two Belgian priests, Lefebvre was summoned to Rome to meet with a commission of cardinals established by Cardinal Villot. By June permission to retain the seminary had been revoked, a decision upheld by the pope.

Matters came to a head with the ordination of priests on June 29. Pope Paul had publicly appealed to Lefebvre during a consistory on May 24, to desist from the priestly ordination. Lefebvre went ahead with the ceremony and was suspended *a divinis*, his faculties to exercise his priesthood withdrawn.

The censure backfired on the pope. Lefebvre was seen as a brave warrior by his supporters and grudgingly admired by many of his critics. On August 29, Archbishop Lefebvre celebrated a Mass in the French city of Lille. An enormous crowd of several thousand listened to his sermon in which he excoriated the pope and the Curia. Paul was deeply troubled by the events. On the day of the ordinations in Ecône, the pope made a private vow never again to eat meat as reparation for the fracture caused in the church.

But the resolution of such difficulties required more than personal sacrifices. In September Lefebvre presented himself at Castel Gandolfo and submitted a short letter requesting to meet with the pope. The prelate had been assured by an intermediary that the pontiff would be willing to meet him. The next morning Lefebvre was received in audience.

In his written account of the meeting, Lefebvre noted that Paul was both nervous and impatient. The encounter started badly when Paul opened by asking the archbishop if he knew the damage his scandal had caused the church. Lefebvre defended himself, pointing to the success of the seminary and parishes served in the traditional manner. He had the impression that Paul took the whole affair personally, noting that the pope appeared stung that the traditionalists flouted his authority. Lefebvre countered that there were enormous abuses in the church that had arisen directly as a result of the council. Paul reluctantly conceded the point, but it was the only point of convergence. Benelli, the *sostituto*, sat silently behind the pope taking notes of the meeting.

Paul was disturbed by the hostile publicity caused by Lefebvre's actions. While he may have sympathized with some of the deviations of which he was well aware, he felt unable to tackle either the proponents of change or the defenders of orthodoxy.

Paul had been exhausted from the increased burdens and public ceremonies demanded by the jubilee year. His arthritis had worsened considerably and he had difficulty with walking. He toyed briefly with the idea of abdicating but the Lefebvre affair complicated the matter. If he should leave the papacy, the traditionalists would see it as a victory and call for the repeal of much of the Second Vatican Council. That would in turn damage the prestige of the papacy as an absolute institution.

As Paul aged the question of the succession increasingly occupied the minds of the cardinals. The appointment of Giovanni Benelli as archbishop of Florence on June 3, 1977, gave the clearest indication of Paul's desire as to whom his successor should be. Benelli had been chief of staff of the Roman Curia for ten years. He worked closely with the pontiff and saw the pope on an almost daily basis. The diocese traditionally carried a cardinal's hat, and three weeks later, Pope Paul made Benelli a cardinal at the consistory of June 27. In his memoirs, Benelli recalled how Paul had wept as he asked his assistant to accept Florence. He knew it was the end of the relationship on which Paul relied. But Paul did not want Benelli excluded from the conclave that would follow his death as he had been when Pius XII died in 1958.

Although popes are prohibited from interfering in the process of their succession, Paul's gesture made abundantly clear his intention. It was evident that this may be the last consistory to be held by Paul, and Benelli's elevation to the Sacred College was an indication of the elderly pontiff's wishes. As no non-Italian had been elected in over four centuries, Benelli was now, although only fifty-seven, the favorite papabile in the event of a vacancy in the Holy See. Benelli's time in Florence, however long it may be, would broaden his pastoral experience and make him an even better papal candidate.

His episcopal motto, *virtus ex alto* (power from on high), provoked wry smiles from several curialists pleased to see his departure from the corridors of the Vatican. Yet none could have foreseen that Benelli would suffer a fatal heart attack in Florence just a few years later at the age of sixty-one.

On August 15, 1977, the pope traveled to a nearby town to bless the newly built Church of Our Lady of the Lake. At the end of a short allocution on the Madonna, Paul spoke unexpectedly about his failing health. In a low and breathless voice he startled his hearers: "Who knows, old as I am, if I will have the opportunity of celebrating with you again this feast day? For I see the threshold of death approaching. Thus I take the opportunity of greeting you all, of blessing your loved ones, your homes, your families, your hopes, your sufferings, that the Madonna hears my prayer that you may all be blessed in her name."[1]

As Paul approached his birthday in September his thoughts turned to the length of life left. Aware that his physical powers were deserting him, he once more considered abdication, the first since 1415. In the event of abdication, he would retire to the Abbey of Montecassino, where a suite awaited him. But he found he had not the strength even to confront the daunting preparations that such an abdication would cause. There seemed little option but to tranquilly await the end of his life in office. As 1978 dawned, few outside the Vatican realized that this would be the last full year of his pontificate. His health, always delicate, remained relatively good for an octogenarian. Apart from painful arthritis, Paul had few difficulties.

In March 1978, the car carrying Aldo Moro, the former Italian prime minister, was hijacked on the Via Fani in Rome. Two cars blocked the entrance and exit of the street. The politician's five bodyguards were gunned down and Moro was kidnapped. Members of the terrorist Red Brigades claimed responsibility, and they demanded the release of sixteen of their members from Italian prisons. The government refused.

Despite a country-wide manhunt for the kidnappers, Moro was held in captivity for almost two months. He was allowed to write to his family and even implored his longtime friend Giovanni Battista Montini to intervene. Paul asked his secretary to contact Don Cesare Curioni, senior chaplain of the state prisons. Despite the risk he ran with the Italian state, Curioni managed to get messages to the Red Brigades. On April 22 Paul made an appeal for the liberation of the politician. The pope begged the kidnappers to release Moro, offering himself in his place. In a letter to his captors he wrote: "On my knees I beg you, free Aldo Moro, simply and without conditions, not so much because of my humble and well-meaning intercession, but because he shares with you the common dignity of a brother in humanity."

Behind the scenes, it seemed as if Curioni had succeeded in obtaining the freedom of the prisoner. On May 8 Curioni visited the pope and indicated that the liberation was due to take place on the morrow. In the early morning of May 9 Don Carlo Cremona, a collaborator of Monsignor Macchi, received a phone call from a contact in the Red Brigades. The caller explained that everything had "gone up in the air," and that the release would not happen. Within hours the Italian State police were informed that Moro had been murdered and given directions to find the corpse at Via Caetani close to Piazza Venezia in Rome. Arriving at the scene, Moro's lifeless body was discovered in the boot of a Renault car.

The news caused consternation in Italy and abroad. The abduction and subsequent murder of Moro had a profound and debilitating effect on Paul. He was devastated by the brutal act and inconsolable at the death of his friend. When a state funeral was arranged to be celebrated on May 13 by Cardinal Ugo Poletti, the vicar for Rome at St. John Lateran, Paul decided to attend. Unable to enter the cathedral by foot, the frail pontiff was carried on the ceremonial *sedia gestatoria*. Clutching his pastoral staff in his gnarled hand, he feebly blessed the crowds. Those who had not seen the pope in public for months were shocked by his morose demeanor and his dramatic loss of weight.

The Mass was unusual in two respects. Neither the corpse was present nor were members of his family. From captivity in April, Moro had written, in the eventuality of his death, that he did not want any politicians present. Notwithstanding the presence of the pope, the Moro family had held the funeral four days earlier in the cemetery of San Tomaso on the outskirts of Rome. At the end of the Mass the pope addressed a rebuke to God on behalf of the mourners: "You have not listened to our prayer, O Lord, for the safe deliverance of Aldo Moro, this good, gentle, wise and innocent friend."

Moro's death prompted Paul to think of his own mortality. In his homily on the feast of St. Peter and St. Paul, June 29, the pope noted that having celebrated his eightieth birthday, it was natural to see his life drawing to a close. At his general audience on July 5, however, Paul seemed in good form, greeting all who were about to begin their period of annual vacation. Advising his listeners to read some good books, he urged them to visit a local sanctuary or make a spiritual retreat of a few days.

It was now time for the pope to leave Rome for his annual summer vacation. The humid weather was insufferable and on July 14 Paul gladly departed for the cooler climate of Castel Gandolfo. The general pace of work continued as ever. Twice each day documentation was sent from the Secretariat of State at the Vatican. Each evening he spent time reading through and initialing pages with suggestions or approval, and on Wednesdays he continued to hold his general audience in the courtyard of the papal villa.

Too tired for excursions, the pope remained in the villa, taking occasional short walks in the gardens. On July 31 he made his final outing from the villa as he went to pray at the tomb of his old companion, Cardinal Giuseppe Pizzardo. The latter had died in 1970 at the age of ninety-three and was buried in nearby Frattocchie. Descending to the crypt, he knelt, with great difficulty, before the sepulchre. On his exit from the church, Professor Mario Fontana, a member of the medical team assigned to the pope, saw that Paul was pale and visibly unwell. Returning to the villa, he examined the pope, who had contracted fever.

Despite medication, the fever did not abate. Against medical advice, the pope insisted on attending the general audience overlooking the courtyard. Although fatigued, Paul worked through the day and retired, as usual, after midnight.

Sandro Pertini, newly elected president of Italy, was to make a courtesy visit the following day. Although the pope was feeble, he insisted on meeting Pertini. The pope was pleased that, although the fever had persisted, the president had not noticed. That evening the pope concluded his day at 11:30 p.m. by praying Compline in his chapel, followed by spiritual reading.

At 2:30 a.m. Paul pressed the bell to call for assistance. When Monsignor Macchi arrived, he found the pope sitting on the bed, gasping for breath. Unable to speak, he gestured to be helped to the armchair, where he took oxygen. On medical advice Paul rested the following day. That night he was unable to sleep and had difficulty breathing. The following morning, Sunday, August 6, Paul remained in bed. In the early afternoon his condition deteriorated, and Dr. Fontana summoned medical assistance. From about 4:00 onward a number of medical personnel began to arrive at the papal villa. With the pope's sudden deterioration, the family was summoned.

Throughout the afternoon the pope drifted in and out of consciousness. At 5:30 his private secretaries concelebrated Mass, after which he was administered the sacrament of anointing of the sick. Cardinal Villot, just arrived from Rome, led the prayers at Paul's bedside. The pope was unable to speak but whispered the prayers of the Our Father and Hail Mary. He closed his eyes and sank into the bed. His vital signs were fading.

Immediately after the Mass, the pope fell into a coma and at 9:40 p.m. he quietly breathed his last.

At the moment of his death, the alarm clock on his bedside table sounded. A gift from his mother in 1923 when he left for Warsaw, the alarm had been inadvertently set the previous day as Monsignor Macchi wound the clock.

Now that my day is drawing to a close, and all of this stupendous and dramatic temporal and earthly scene is ending and dissolving, how can I further thank thee, O Lord, after the gift of natural life, also for the higher gift of faith and grace, in which alone at the end my surviving existence finds refuge?

(Last Will and Testament of Paul VI)

Epilogue

On August 25, 1978, the cardinal-electors gathered in the Sistine Chapel to choose a successor to Pope Paul. Although the largest number of electors to hitherto participate in a conclave, fifteen cardinals over eighty were excluded according to the regulations introduced by the late pontiff. The next afternoon, on the fourth ballot of the conclave, Cardinal Albino Luciani, patriarch of Venice, was elected. He had obtained in excess of the required two-thirds majority for election. The new pope took the name John Paul in honor of his two immediate predecessors.

Although he had occupied the prestigious See of Venice for nineteen years, Luciani was little known outside Italy. The cardinals chose a candidate known for his holiness and humility. These qualities immediately endeared him to the public in his first appearances. Dubbed the "smiling pope" by the media in contrast to the grim face of Paul's later years, Luciani was also theologically conservative.

There was little time to discover what direction his pontificate would take, as he died suddenly on the night of September 28. For the second time in a month the cardinals reassembled to elect a new pope. This time they chose the fifty-eight-year-old archbishop of Krakow, Karol Wojtyla, the first Slavic pope.

The new pope took the name John Paul II in tribute to his short-lived predecessor. During his twenty-seven-year pontificate John Paul imprinted his personality on the church. A former university professor of moral philosophy, John Paul was a strict disciplinarian. He censored theologians whose writings conflicted with traditional church teaching. His athletic figure, impish sense of humor, and pleasant personal demeanor did not hide his uncompromising stance on morality but made him immensely popular with a large number of people, Catholic and non-Catholic alike.

With extraordinary energy, Pope John Paul undertook over two hundred international visits during his pontificate, covering over 700,000 miles. These visits raised the international prestige of the papacy. The most controversial issue of the early part of his pontificate revolved around the position of women in the church (refusing the possibility of ordination of women to the ordained ministry). The later years, dogged by increasing frailty due to Parkinson's disease, were overshadowed by the public disclosure of clerical pedophilia and cover-ups, as well as rapidly spreading secularization. Ecumenism continued to slowly develop under Pope John Paul. The enthusiasm of the council gave way to entrenched stubbornness on each side of the Christian divide as well as a realization that Christianity was so disparate that global unity was no longer a realistic goal. Relations with other world religions developed on the lines of mutual respect for each other's traditions.

Shortly after his death in 2005, John Paul II was succeeded by the German-born Cardinal Joseph Ratzinger, a professional theologian who had spent twenty-three years at the Vatican overseeing theological issues. Although not as outgoing as the Polish pope, Pope Benedict XVI continued the innovations of the council that Paul had closed forty years earlier. Pope Benedict had taken part in the council as a theological expert. Continuing the apostolic voyages initiated by Paul VI and sustained by John Paul II, Pope Benedict also tried to restore elements of the Roman liturgy that had been replaced in the aftermath of the council.

Citing age and diminished health, Pope Benedict abdicated on February 28, 2013. He was succeeded after a two-day conclave by the Latin-American Jesuit archbishop of Buenos Aires. The initial task of the first pope from the Americas was to lead the church that had increasingly suffered from public scandals of sexual abuse by clergy and financial corruption. Pope Francis's focus was immediately on the poor and disenfranchised and he championed migrants and those caught up in human trafficking.

It was Pope Francis who brought to a conclusion the twenty-one-year investigation into the possibility of beatifying Pope Paul. A miracle was required for public recognition. In 2013 a commission of medics and theologians at the Vatican accepted the miraculous healing of an unborn child who suffered congenital defects and whose mother had been advised by doctors to have an abortion. The mother prayed through the intercession of Pope Paul for the safe delivery of her baby. The child was born without defects.

During the homily at the beatification ceremony held in St. Peter's Square on October 19, 2014, Pope Francis quoted some words written by Pope Paul: "Perhaps the Lord has called me and preserved me for this service not because I am particularly fit for it, or so that I can govern and rescue the Church from her present difficulties, but so that I can suffer something for the Church, and in that way it will be clear that he, and no other, is her guide and saviour."[1]

Beatification is the penultimate step toward canonization and one further miracle is required before the final step. The miracle attributed to the intercession of Blessed Paul concerned an Italian woman from Verona, Vanna Pironato, who began to lose amniotic fluid from her womb early in her pregnancy. She went to the shrine of Our Lady of Graces at Brescia and prayed to God, through the intercession of Blessed Paul, that her unborn child would survive.

Although the medics feared that the child would not live, the infant Amanda was born healthy in 2014. The medical team had no scientific explanation for how the child had survived.

The process of canonization examines the life of a Christian and declares that the person lived a virtuous life worthy of imitation. Paul lived an extraordinary life of intense dedication to Christ, often in the face of adversity. Whatever his human failings, the church now turns to him in heaven as a beacon of faith.

Notes

Preface—pages vii–viii

1. The Testament of Paul VI, *L'Osservatore Romano*, August 24, 1978, https://w2.vatican.va/content/paul-vi/en/speeches/1978/august/documents/hf_p-vi_spe_19780810_testamento-paolo-vi.html.

Chapter Three: Pius XII, the Postwar Years, and the Departure for Milan—pages 30–51

1. David Dalin, *The Pius War: Responses to the Critics of Pius XII*, ed. Joseph Bottum and David Dalin (Lanham, MD: Lexington, 2004), 18.

2. Jean Guitton, *The Pope Speaks* (New York: Meredith Press, 1968), 26.

Chapter Four: John XXIII, the Council, and the Election of John Baptist—pages 52–70

1. In conversation with the author in Bergamo, Italy, in 2014.

2. Solemn Opening of the Second Vatican Council, October 11, 1962, http://w2.vatican.va/content/john-xxiii/it/speeches/1962/documents/hf_j-xxiii_spe_19621011_opening-council.html (author's translation).

3. Greeting of John XXIII on the Opening of the Second Vatican Council, October 11, 1962, http://w2.vatican.va/content/john-xxiii

/it/speeches/1962/documents/hf_j-xxiii_spe_19621011_luna.html
(author's translation).

Chapter Five: The Missionary Pope—pages 71–93

1. Solemn Closing of the Second Vatican Council, December 4,
1963, http://w2.vatican.va/content/paul-vi/it/speeches/1963
/documents/hf_p-vi_spe_19631204_chiusura-concilio.html (author's
translation).

2. Homily at "Mass of the Artists" in the Sistine Chapel, May 7,
1964, http://w2.vatican.va/content/paul-vi/it/homilies/1964
/documents/hf_p-vi_hom_19640507_messa-artisti.html (author's
translation).

3. Address to the United Nations, October 4, 1965, http://w2
.vatican.va/content/paul-vi/en/speeches/1965/documents/hf_p-vi
_spe_19651004_united-nations.html.

4. Address to the Conciliar Fathers Regarding His Visit to the UN,
October 5, 1965, http://w2.vatican.va/content/paul-vi/it/speeches
/1965/documents/hf_p-vi_spe_19651005_resoconto-viaggio.html
(author's translation).

5. *Wall Street Journal* (March 30, 1967): "Pope Paul's encyclical
lends the mantle of religion to certain ideas which are profoundly
secular in origin, *and advocates programs of a type now undergoing
widespread reappraisal by their one-time secular sponsors. . . . The
trouble with making religious tenets of this souped-up Marxism is*
that it is highly unlikely to help the bulk of poor nations (which)
suffer not from an excess of capitalism, but from a paucity of it. . . .
It is both curious and sad that these mistaken attitudes toward foreign
aid should now be advanced from the realm of religion. For the realm
of history, as more people are starting to recognize, shows that they
impede rather than advance the development of peoples." *The Econo-
mist* (April 8, 1967) gave a more balanced view, noting that "some
Communists who hailed it ignored its flat condemnation of materi-
alistic ideologies."

6. Speech at Cathedral of the Holy Spirit, Istanbul, July 25, 1967,
http://w2.vatican.va/content/paul-vi/fr/speeches/1967/july/documents

/hf_p-vi_spe_19670725_cattedrale-spirito-santo.html (author's translation).

7. Pasquale Macchi, "The Pope in the Holy Land," *30 Days*, issue 2 (2000).

Chapter Six: Paul and the Postconciliar Church— pages 94–122

1. Holy Mass for the Campesinos Colombiani, August 23, 1968, https://w2.vatican.va/content/paul-vi/it/homilies/1968/documents /hf_p-vi_hom_19680823.html (author's translation).

2. Message of Paul VI on the Occasion of the Lunar Undertaking, July 21, 1969, https://w2.vatican.va/content/paul-vi/it/speeches/1969 /july/documents/hf_p-vi_spe_19690721_impresa-lunare.html (author's translation).

3. General audience, November 26, 1969, https://w2.vatican.va /content/paul-vi/it/audiences/1969/documents/hf_p-vi_aud_19691126 .html (author's translation).

4. Address, Apostolic Pilgrimage in Eastern Asia, Oceania and Australia, November 26, 1970, http://w2.vatican.va/content/paul-vi /it/speeches/1970/documents/hf_p-vi_spe_19701126_aeroporto-da -vinci.html (author's translation).

5. Homily, Apostolic Pilgrimage to West Asia, Oceania and Australia, November 28, 1970, https://w2.vatican.va/content/paul-vi/en /homilies/1970/documents/hf_p-vi hom_19701128.html.

6. Homily, Apostolic Pilgrimage to West Asia, Oceania and Australia, November 29, 1970, https://w2.vatican.va/content/paul-vi/en /homilies/1970/documents/hf_p-vi_hom_19701129.html.

7. Homily on the Ninth Anniversary of the Pontificate of His Holiness, June 29, 1972, http://w2.vatican.va/content/paul-vi/it /homilies/1972/documents/hf_p-vi_hom_19720629.html (author's translation).

8. Homily, Concelebration with Italian Bishops, June 8, 1974, https://w2.vatican.va/content/paul-vi/it/homilies/1974/documents /hf_p-vi_hom_19740608.html (author's translation).

Chapter Seven: A Pontificate Drawing to a Close— pages 123–32

1. Peter Hebblethwaite, *Paul VI: The First Modern Pope* (Mahwah, NJ: Paulist Press, 1993), 684.

Epilogue—pages 133–36

1. Homily of Pope Francis at the Closing Mass of the Extraordinary Synod on the Family and Beatification of Paul VI, October 19, 2014, https://w2.vatican.va/content/francesco/en/homilies/2014/documents/papa-francesco_20141019_omelia-chiusura-sinodo -beatificazione-paolo-vi.html.